6

WORDS THAT WILL CHANGE YOUR LIFE

GOD. OUR. SINS. PAYING. EVERYONE. LIFE.

40 DAY DEVOTIONAL

GREG STIER

DARE 2 SHARE

6 Words That Will Change Your Life

Copyright © 2015 Dare 2 Share Ministries.
All rights reserved.

A D2S Publishing book
PO Box 745323
Arvada, CO 80006

This devotional may be used independently from or in conjunction with the video series *Life in 6 Words: The GOSPEL Explored*.

Editor: Jane Dratz

Stier, Greg
6 Words That Will Change Your Life

ISBN: 978-0-9960178-0-0
Library of Congress Control Number: 2014951110
Printed in the United States of America

DEDICATION

To Propaganda (AKA Jason Petty)

The spoken word poem you wrote
for Dare 2 Share
has inspired a movement of
Gospel Advancing Ministries!

TABLE OF CONTENTS

PAYING the Price for Sin, Jesus Died and Rose Again

EVERYONE Who Trusts in Him Has Eternal Life

LIFE with Jesus Starts Now and Lasts Forever

INTRODUCTION

How can six words change your life?

Because these six words represent six truths that make up the core essentials of the gospel message.

God created us to be with Him.

Our sins separate us from God.

Sins cannot be removed by good deeds.

Paying the price for sin, Jesus died and rose again.

Everyone who trusts in Him alone has eternal life.

Life with Jesus starts now and lasts forever.

When you let the message of the gospel sink deep into your soul, it draws you further and further into God's love, bringing healing and wholeness. When you extend this message to those around you who don't know Jesus, its grace and truth can blast them out of the kingdom of darkness and into His marvelous light.

Although this message is 2,000 years old, it feels brand new. Its message is more relevant than ever. Here's a checklist of just some of the struggles that understanding and embracing the gospel tackles:

- Bad self image…Why? We have been declared a new creation! 2 Corinthians 5:17
- Guilt…How? Jesus paid the price for all of our sins! Colossians 2:13

- Sin's power…When? The power of sin was crushed when Jesus was! Romans 6:6
- Bitterness…How? We can forgive others because Jesus forgave us! Ephesians 4:32
- Spiritual apathy…Why? We offer ourselves to Him in light of His sacrifice! Romans 12:1

On and on and on the list goes! The gospel is so powerful and practical that I'm convinced of this radical premise: IF CHRISTIANS MASTER AND ARE MASTERED BY THE GOSPEL MESSAGE, THEY WILL BE WAY MORE LIKELY TO SERVE JESUS WITH PASSION AND PURPOSE!!!

That's why each devo reading in this book includes a Life Application section. These daily practical applications are designed to either move the message of the gospel deeper into your own soul, or prompt you to take the gospel wider into your world.

Granted, some of you may find the exercises that prompt you to share the gospel with others intimidating, but let me encourage you to step up to this challenge. I realize there are many excuses that tug us in the opposite direction of embracing this challenge. Our lives are busy. Our inadequacies overwhelm us. Our hearts are hardened to the lost, and we just don't care. And some of us are just plain scared out of our wits at the prospect of sharing our faith.

But I'm convinced that as we increasingly focus on God's immense love for us, talking about Jesus with others can become a mindset we live, rather than a "duty" we shrink from and feel guilty about ducking.

Scripture makes it clear that God has called all of us as His followers to the privilege of telling others about His incredible, free gift of eternal life available in Christ. The Apostle Paul puts it this way in 2 Corinthians 5:14; 18-20,

For Christ's love compels us, because we are convinced that one died for all, and therefore all died...All this is from God, who reconciled us to himself through Christ and gave us the ministry of reconciliation: that God was reconciling the world to himself in Christ, not counting people's sins against them. And he has committed to us the message of reconciliation. We are therefore Christ's ambassadors, as though God were making his appeal through us. We implore you on Christ's behalf: Be reconciled to God.

So ask God to help you more and more fully live in the center of Christ's love for you, until like Paul, *"Christ's love compels"* you to tell others about it. Ask Him to give you a heart that increasingly burns and breaks for the lost. Start there, and watch what He does in and through you. You'll grow more and more compassionate, capable and confident as you hold out the gift of life.

The gift of LIFE in six words. God. Our. Sins. Paying. Everyone. Life.

A SPECIAL NOTE TO READERS

This devotional may be used independently from or in conjunction with the video series *Life in 6 Words: The GOSPEL Explored.* However, if you've never seen the virally popular YouTube video *Life in 6 Words*, that serves as a companion to this devotional, I encourage you take a moment and watch it now. You can find it at lifein6words.com. The video breathes life and power into the simple message of the gospel as it unpacks life in six words.

GOD

CREATED US
TO BE WITH HIM

Know that the Lord is God.
It is he who made us, and we are his.

- Psalm 100:3a

01 THE ORIGINAL G

In the beginning God created the heavens and the earth. Genesis 1:1

Then God said, "Let us make mankind in our image, in our likeness, so that they may rule over the fish in the sea and the birds in the sky, over the livestock and all the wild animals, and over all the creatures that move along the ground." Genesis 1:26

"Where did I come from?" "Who is my Daddy?" "Why am I here?"

These are the kinds of questions that plagued my brain growing up. Raised in a rough, tough, high crime Denver neighborhood, I longed for something more than the chaos that surrounded me.

Having never met by biological father, a whole array of Daddy issues tangled within my soul. I was a pensive, quiet kid who used a flashlight to read my Bible while sitting underneath the kitchen sink, or in a closet, or under my bed.

I was trying to get away from the noise of my very loud, very violent, very angry family. Mom was angry, because she had to raise two boys on her own. My brother was angry, because of how kids made fun of him for his epilepsy and struggles in school. My extended family members, including my grandfather and lots of aunts, uncles and cousins, wrestled with a simmering rage that could explode instantly into flying fists and bloody violence.

The organized crime ringleaders in Denver referred to my five uncles as "the crazy brothers." When the mafia thinks your family is dysfunctional, something is definitely wrong. All the family violence, added to the confusion of what life was all about for me as a kid.

I remember reading Genesis 1 in the little red King James Version Bible that Mrs. Murehead gave me. I read that *"in the beginning God created the heavens and the earth"* and something struck a chord in my searching young soul.

There was a bigger reason for life than making money, paying bills and throwing fists. My little red Bible assured me that although my uncles were built like Neanderthals, their existence was not a result of random chance. Instead, they were handcrafted by God Himself—the Original G.

God invites us into His power and presence.

In Genesis 1, the Bible tells us that from the very beginning, God invited us humans into His power and presence. God literally created us to be with Him! When He said, *"Let us make mankind in our image…,"* we see a conspiracy within the Trinity to create humanity in such a way that we can relate with Him deeply and personally.

The Father engineered us (Psalm 139:13-14). Jesus made us (John 1:1-3). And the Holy Spirit empowered the entire process (Genesis 1:2). From the beginning of time, we were made to be in intimate fellowship with every member of the Trinity.

The members of the Trinity were in perfect fellowship with each other and perfectly fine without us. God didn't create us because He was lonely. The Father, Son and Holy Spirit had perfect love for and fellowship with each other. They were not lonely. They were one—perfectly united in a way that our puny, finite minds can never comprehend.

But they created us to invite us into that perfect fellowship they share—though I want to be clear here that while we are invited into fellowship with the Trinity, we will never be members of the Trinity itself.

Jesus prayed to the Father in John 17:24, *"Father, I want those you have given me to be with me where I am, and to see my glory, the glory you have given me because you loved me before the creation of the world."*

We have access into the same ocean of love.

It's through Christ's shed blood, that we have access into the same ocean of love that pulsates between the Father, Son and Holy Spirit. Ephesians 3:17-19 puts it this way, *"And I pray that you, being rooted and established in love, may have power, together with all the Lord's holy people, to grasp how wide and long and high and deep is the love of Christ, and to know this love that surpasses knowledge—that you may be filled to the measure of all the fullness of God."*

This amazing theological truth gave me hope as a child that, not only was I loved, but I was not alone, after all. There was a bigger purpose. There was a larger Being. And this Supreme Being loved me with an everlasting love.

Guess what? This same God wants to be in relationship with you, too.

LIFE APPLICATION

Stop and consider the love that God has for you. Think about the reality that God created you to be in a relationship with Him. The Father, Son and Holy Spirit are inviting you into a relationship with them, through Jesus.

IF YOU'VE NEVER TRUSTED IN CHRIST

Have you put your faith in Jesus to save you, based on His death on the cross for your sins and His resurrection from the dead? If not, what's holding you back? The moment you trust in Jesus, you enter into an eternal relationship with the Triune God. Your life will never be the same. Both now and for all eternity.

While saying a prayer isn't what gets you into a relationship with God, it is a way for you to express your newfound faith. You might pray something like this...

> **"Dear God, I know that my sins have broken my relationship with You, and that nothing I could do could ever change that. But right now, I believe that Jesus died in my place, and rose again from the dead. I trust in Him to forgive me for my sins. Through faith in Him, I am entering an eternal relationship with You. Thank You for this free gift! Amen."**

IF YOU'RE ALREADY A CHRISTIAN

If you are already a believer in Jesus, are you experiencing the love of the Trinity in your own life? Think of an area of hurt, struggle or disappointment in your life where you sometimes feel like you are all alone. Invite the Trinity into that space. Then re-read Ephesians 3:17-19, mentioned above, but this time, read it as a personal prayer. Ask God to encircle you in His love.

02 BIG BANG BADA BING

And God said, *"Let there be light"* and there was light. Genesis 1:3

In the beginning was the Word, and the Word was with God, and the Word was God. He was with God in the beginning. Through him all things were made; without him nothing was made that has been made. John 1:1-3

Scientists argue, theologians debate, apologists apologize (just kidding), but the creation act was way more impressive and complex than any scientist or theology prof can ever fully comprehend or explain.

When God said, "Let there be light," there was light. When He said, "Let there be sky," there was sky. When He said, "Let there be…water, land, trees, fish, birds, bugs, animals, anything and almost everything," there it was. His words spoke creation into existence.

He speaks, and "BANG" it happens.

God is the only being in this universe who can speak something from nothing. He speaks, and "BANG" it happens.

I'll never forget one time when I was in fourth grade, and I was trying to speak my own reality into existence. I ran in the dirt field in the back of our apartment complex, determined to fly like Superman. I thought, "If I can believe it hard enough, then I can make it happen." So I began to run, jump and chant to myself, "Fly. Fly! Fly!!!"

In the end, I just looked like a crazy kid running and jumping through an empty field with my arms extended forward. More than once, I ended up face-first in the dirt.

Yes, I got beat up a lot as a kid.

But try as I might, I couldn't speak my own reality into existence. Nobody but Jesus can do that!

According to Colossians 1:15-20, this "speaking-something-from-nothing" ability is true of God's nature, not just when it comes to physical realities, but also spiritual ones. *"The Son is the image of the invisible God, the firstborn over all creation. For in him all things were created: things in heaven and on earth, visible and invisible, whether thrones or powers or rulers or authorities; all things have been created through him and for him. He is before all things, and in him all things hold together. And he is the head of the body, the church; he is the beginning and the firstborn from among the dead, so that in everything he might have the supremacy. For God was pleased to have all his fullness dwell in him, and through him to reconcile to himself all things, whether things on earth or things in heaven, by making peace through his blood, shed on the cross."*

He created heaven and hell. He created angels (some of whom would become demons). He created the visible things that we see every day, and the invisible ones which we don't see, but that are just as much a reality.

Not only is He the Creator, He is the Sustainer (*"in him all things hold together"*) and Ruler (*"so that in everything he might have the supremacy."*)

From the first chapter of Genesis, to the last chapter of Revelation, God is large and in charge. He is in charge of the creation and He is in charge of salvation. 2 Corinthians

God is large and in charge.

4:6 makes it clear, *"For God, who said, 'Let light shine out of darkness,' made his light shine in our hearts to give us the light of the knowledge of God's glory displayed in the face of Christ."*

The same God who said, *"Let there be light"* in the act of the universe's creation said, *"Let there be light"* in the act of your spiritual regeneration. He illuminated your soul and blasted you out of the kingdom of darkness into the kingdom of his dear Son (Colossians 1:13).

When God speaks, powerful things happen. Universes explode into existence, and souls are eternally transformed. That's one reason it's important to take his Word—The Bible—seriously. As you read it and let it sink into your soul, His Word will create new realities in your life!

Bada Boom!

LIFE APPLICATION

Consider once again this powerful description of Jesus in Colossians 1:15-17: *"The Son is the image of the invisible God, the firstborn over all creation. For in him all things were created: things in heaven and on earth, visible and invisible, whether thrones or powers or rulers or authorities; all things have been created through him and for him. He is before all things, and in him all things hold together."*

Meditate on this passage about Jesus, then take a look at your attitudes and actions and consider whether you are living like you really believe that God is large and in charge. Are you busy stressing and striving and trying to "control" every aspect of your life? Or are you learning to rest in His sovereignty and be content in all things, knowing that come what may, *"in him all things hold together"*?

03 GOD'S MUDDY, SMILING FACE

Then the Lord God formed a man from the dust of the ground and breathed into his nostrils the breath of life, and the man became a living being. Genesis 2:7

As a latchkey kid, I watched a lot of *Mr. Rogers Neighborhood* while I waited for my mom to get home from work. I'll never forget one of the simple little songs he sang over and over, *It's You I Like.*

> It's you I like,
> It's not the things you wear,
> It's not the way you do your hair--
> But it's you I like.
> The way you are right now,
> The way down deep inside you...[1]

For thirty minutes, Mr. Rogers would remind me and millions of other children across the nation how special we were. He told us through goofy sketches and imaginary characters that we were unique, and ended each program by saying, "You've made this day a special day by just your being you. There's no person in the whole world like you. And I like you just the way you are."[2] Maybe that's why so many kids watched the show. We needed to hear that. We needed to know that.

But as children turn into teenagers, and teenagers morph into adults, this message often fades. In its place, feelings of failure can creep in, bringing a sinister, understated hatred for what we see in the mirror and feel in our souls. In fact, Mister Rogers reported that he'd heard from countless people struggling with self-image problems, depression or loneliness. These hurting souls told him that as adults, they had happened across his program while channel surfing, and had stayed tuned in, because they found acceptance, love and hope in his simple message.

"I like you just the way you are."

In the previous devo reading, I mentioned that God spoke "almost everything" into existence. This is true, with one glaring exception…the first man, Adam. God made Adam special.

Imagine the second Person of the Trinity, the Son of God Himself, walking in the midst of His new creation. Maybe He patted the head of a hippopotamus, scratched the back of a silverback gorilla and allowed an eagle to alight on His shoulder. But, as He surveyed His good creation, there was something that was missing that would make it "very good." That something was humanity.

So, on the sixth day of creation, God dropped knee-first into the water-drenched mud of the earth and began to make a sculpture. He used His bare hands to handcraft a special creation, unlike anything else He had spoken into existence.

Perhaps the angels—maybe even Lucifer—was watching from a distance, as God did something He had never done before…get dirty.

Imagine God, covered in mud, having formed His mud man just right. But, being still a lifeless form, He knelt down even closer to the part of the wet dirt that resembled a nose and breathed into it His own divine breath.

This holy exhale infused life into the form, turning minerals into cells, dust into bones and mud into muscle. Suddenly before God, right underneath His face, is a man made in His own image. A man who in many ways, but not every way, was like Him.

Maybe Adam coughed and rubbed his newly formed eyes, but the first thing he saw, when his virgin eyelids opened, was the smiling muddy face of God Himself. Here was his mud-stained Creator hovering over him face-to-face, eye-to-eye, instantly demonstrating the intimacy between Creator and created.

Have you ever questioned why God made you with the characteristics that He did? Maybe there's something about yourself that you don't particularly like. I remember having a zit problem in high school. I looked in the mirror and didn't like what I saw, so I got the magic medicine called "tetracycline." It helped to clear up my acne problem, but it didn't clean up my poor self-image.

Having been a bookworm, raised in a family full of bodybuilders, I was extremely self-conscious, and wrestled with my self-image. So ultimately, I didn't need tetracycline (or weight training, for that matter), I needed a dose of the truth that God made me to be me. I needed the prescription found in Psalm 139:13-14: *"For you created my inmost being; you knit me together in my mother's womb. I praise you because I am fearfully and wonderfully made; your works are wonderful, I know that full well."*

Just imagine the smiling face of God.

Although we all know where babies come from (hopefully), maybe something you didn't know is that a micro act of creation happens every time a new life is conceived. In a mysterious process of the hand of God combining with His established laws of nature, God handcrafts every new life in the womb of his or her mother. Can't you just imagine the smiling face of God looking down from heaven every time a new life is conceived?

As a result, you are *"fearfully and wonderfully made,"* just the way you are. It doesn't matter if you're a bookworm or a bodybuilder, short or tall, fat or skinny, acne-filled or acne-free. God made you to be you in the womb of your momma.

Animals are cool—no doubt about it. Our family has a lizard named Einstein and a wiener dog named Patches. But, at the end of the day, our fellow humans are much more valuable, because it's only humans who were handcrafted by God and infused with a soul through His divine breath. It's only humankind who reflects the nature of God Himself on so many levels.

You are special, not just because Mr. Rogers says you are, but because God made you just the way you are.

LIFE APPLICATION

Imagine God smiling over each and every person He created—including you! Let the truth that God loves you "just the way you are" sink into your soul for a few quiet moments. Then as you walk through your next 24 hours, be a people watcher. Pray for each person you encounter. Pray that those who don't know Christ personally would be reunited with their Creator through the salvation Jesus offers.

04 "WHOA-MAN!"

So the man gave names to all the livestock, the birds in the sky and all the wild animals.

But for Adam no suitable helper was found. So the Lord God caused the man to fall into a deep sleep; and while he was sleeping, he took one of the man's ribs and then closed up the place with flesh. Then the Lord God made a woman from the rib he had taken out of the man, and he brought her to the man.

The man said,
"This is now bone of my bones
*   and flesh of my flesh;*
she shall be called 'woman,'
*   for she was taken out of man."*

That is why a man leaves his father and mother and is united to his wife, and they become one flesh. (Genesis 2:20-24)

Don't you just love it?!? Matchmaking God's way.

If you've ever been through the emotional ups and downs of searching for that special someone, I'm sure you can appreciate the beauty and simplicity of this very first match made in heaven. No need for Tinder or match.com. No false starts, missteps or bruised egos.

This was nothing like my awkward dating experiences throughout my high school and college years, when I tried to talk the various girls who caught my interest into going out with me—with varying degrees of success. During my single years, a trail of polite dodges, and at times, outright rejections, followed in my wake. Until in His perfect time, God brought the *real* girl of my dreams into my life. She was gorgeous *and* godly. All those years of striving melted away when I realized that God had actually been protecting me from a marriage misstep with the wrong woman. When the time was right, God maneuvered me down a path that led me to my wonderful wife.

Of course, my future wife still needed to be convinced that I was the right guy. But after I pulled the competition aside and threatened them with physical harm if they didn't exit the scene quietly, things came to a happy conclusion, and she finally said "Yes!" Yet, God had His purposes in making me wait.

Did you notice in today's passage that after God created Adam, He made him wait for a bit before He brought Adam's female counterpart onto the scene? Perhaps so Adam would appreciate Eve all the more. Maybe this contributed to Adam's enthusiastic response when he first saw Eve and declared, "She shall be called 'Whoa-man!'" (my paraphrase).

Loneliness was never God's intent for humans.

In His own perfect timing, God rolled out His relational plan for the very first man and woman. He provided the helpmate Adam's heart longed for in Eve.

One of the core spiritual truths we can take away from this passage is that loneliness was never God's intent for humans. Our God is relational in His Triune nature. And because you're created in His image, you're relational too. God hard-wired Adam for deep, intimate, personal relationship—with Him and with another human—which means you're hard-wired that way too.

Headlines about loneliness sometimes hit the news. Psychologists express concern that we're becoming increasingly emotionally isolated in our wired, virtual world of "Friends, Fans and Followers." In fact, studies show that emotional isolation is ranked as high a risk factor for mortality as smoking and obesity.[3]

We humans are designed for relational connection. We see this truth laid out in Scripture from Genesis to Revelations—from God's perfect intent for us in the Garden of Eden, to the God-ordained collective nature of the Church as the Bride of Christ, to the glimpses we see of a heaven where together we'll corporately gather in worship around the throne of God.

God designed us to be in relationship with Him and with each other.

We're designed for relational connection.

If you're married, this passage in Genesis 2 also lays out another key spiritual truth which is a bedrock principle for a healthy marriage—leaving and cleaving. Isn't it interesting that God moved the writer of Genesis to include this critical marriage principle here, prominently inserting it into the narrative that depicts the launch of the very first husband-wife relationship? Especially given the reality that Adam and had no father or mother to leave. God's telling us married folk something important here about what makes the marriage relationship work the way He originally designed it—an unwavering commitment to being "one."

Think of it! God was the very first matchmaker AND the very first marriage counselor.

LIFE APPLICATION

We live in a culture where it's easy to be lonely, even when we're surrounded by people. But as believers, we need never feel truly lonely, because our relationship with God reaches down into the deepest part of our soul. Psalm 42:1 says: *"As the deer pants for streams of water, so my soul pants for you, my God."*

Does your soul pant for God? If not, ask Him to stir in you a hunger and thirst to know and love Him better. If so, spend a few quiet moments drinking in His presence and experiencing Him as the Living Water.

05 "LET THERE BE...WORK?"

God blessed them and said to them, "Be fruitful and increase in number; fill the earth and subdue it. Rule over the fish in the sea and the birds in the sky and over every living creature that moves on the ground."

Then God said, "I give you every seed-bearing plant on the face of the whole earth and every tree that has fruit with seed in it. They will be yours for food. And to all the beasts of the earth and all the birds in the sky and all the creatures that move along the ground—everything that has the breath of life in it—I give every green plant for food." And it was so. Genesis 1:28-30

The Lord God took the man and put him in the Garden of Eden to work it and take care of it. Genesis 2:15

Lots of people think that work is one of the unfortunate consequences of the Fall, something that descended upon us humans after Adam and Eve got themselves kicked out of the Garden of Eden. But these passages tell us otherwise.

Work was part of God's intentions for us from the very start—work that was ordained by Him and held meaning and purpose, that is.

"Be fruitful and increase in number..." For anyone who's ever had children, that statement alone is clearly a recipe for work. Our offspring are a joy and delight, but they are also a lot of work—round the clock feedings, making sure they don't eat dirt or run around with sticks in their mouths, and so on.

Work was part of God's intentions for us from the very start.

Of course, back in the Garden there would have been no sibling spats to negotiate…but you get my point—the kids would still need care and nurture.

And that's just the kids! God's assignment for us human before the Fall goes way beyond making babies and raising them.

Subdue the earth…rule over all the living creatures…work the Garden and take care of it. Granted, there were no weeds before the Fall, but still, God used the word "work" for a reason.

So why did He give us work to do? Because we are created in His image and He's a creative, purposeful God. As God laid out the foundations of the world, Scripture tells us that He was at work. *"By the seventh day God had finished the work he had been doing; so on the seventh day he rested from all his work. Then God blessed the seventh day and made it holy, because on it he rested from all the work of creating that he had done"* (Genesis 2:2-3).

In the creation account, we even see God repeatedly assessing His work, making sure that it was good and taking pleasure in His good work.

God created us to get pleasure from expressing our creativity, from our accomplishments, and from finding purpose and meaning in the tasks He's given us to do. It's true that after the Fall, the nature of work changed…more on that later. But even in our broken world, we get a certain satisfaction from solving problems, being creative, building things and doing a job well.

Now you may be thinking, "Easy for you to talk about the satisfaction of work, you've never had the kind of crappy job I'm stuck in." Let me disabuse you of that thought.

He's a creative, purposeful God.

My first job was as a hay hauler, repetitively working 12 hour days, 6 days a week in the blazing hot sun of the panhandle of Texas. My second job was as a roofer, repetitively stapling shingles in the blazing sun on a hot roof. My third job was as a pizza delivery driver, repetitively building pizza boxes in a hot kitchen and delivering pizzas to hungry, impatient customers. My fourth job was as a UPS guy, once again under the gun of quotas and deadlines.

From the world's perspective, none of these jobs was very fun, but I strived to keep my head down and work hard. Why? Because of the Apostle Paul words in Colossians 3:23-24, *"Whatever you do, work at it with all your heart, as working for the Lord, not for human masters, since you know that you will receive an inheritance from the Lord as a reward. It is the Lord Christ you are serving."*

So in the midst of the daily grind of work, whether on the job, on the home front or as a volunteer laborer in Christ's church, never lose sight of the truth that work was ordained by God way back in the Garden before the Fall.

LIFE APPLICATION

Does your attitude toward work need a recalibration, in order to come into alignment with God's original intent for the role of work in your life?

Whether your a student, on the job or on the home front, talk to God about your work responsibilities today. Make a conscious effort today to purposefully give your work to Him. Do it *"with all your heart, as working for the Lord, not for human masters."*

06 NAKED AND LOVING IT

Adam and his wife were both naked, and they felt no shame. Genesis 2:25

There's something about being naked that makes me blush. Even the word kinda makes me blush. "Nude" seems crude. Why is that?

One hot summer's day in 1980, I went to the movie theatre with my friend. I was fifteen years old, and in that awkward stage of life where I was self-aware and self-conscious.

As we stood outside the theatre looking at the movie posters, I noticed a long line of high school-aged girls getting tickets. So I flexed my puny arms that were extending outside the holes of my tank top tee shirt, and tried to show them a little tricep as I pointed to our various movie options.

Problem was, my spastic friend, Art, who was a prankster at heart, was standing right behind me. I was wearing shorts, and in one swift motion, Art pulled my shorts completely down to the ground and I was standing there exposed. I suppose you could say I was instantly angelic…low and behold.

Instead of pulling my shorts back up, I tried to run…which turned out even worse for me and for everyone watching.

Why do we giggle when we hear the words "nudist beach"? Why do we cringe at the thought of losing our swim suit on a water slide?

It all goes back to the Garden of Eden.

Before the Fall of humanity, Adam and Eve were naked and loving it. They had nothing to hide, both literally and figuratively. They were unashamed of their bodies. They looked at themselves as magnificent creations of an even more magnificent God. Plus, because God "don't make no junk," they likely had no physical blemishes. In a very real way, they were perfect specimens.

They had nothing to hide before God, or each other, for that matter. Their slates were clean, and their hearts were pure. Their thoughts hovered between good and grateful.

They had nothing to hide before God or each other.

Adam loved Eve. Eve Loved Adam. Both of them loved God.

This pure and utter transparency was God's original intent for all of humanity. Nakedness was beauty not lost on lust. They experienced pure, unfiltered conversation from the deepest chamber of each other's hearts and minds. There was, literally, nothing to hide.

I think we all long for this deepest level of honesty and openness with God and each other. Down deep inside we want it, but it feels like we have to get naked to get it. And we do. Sometimes.

In our best moments, we go naked before God, refusing to hide behind religion or excuses, letting down our defenses. We get transparent with our loved ones, and share with them our struggles and insecurities.

When we can live in this level of transparency, it transports us back to the Garden of God, and allows us a taste of the authenticity that was the norm, before sin and shame ruined everything.

We all long for this deepest level of honesty.

But it's just a taste…for now.

Someday, Jesus will make all things new, and we'll be back to that pre-Fall level of authenticity and transparency with God and each other. Check out what the Apostle John has to say about this future state, *"And I heard a loud voice from the throne saying, 'Look! God's dwelling place is now among the people, and he will dwell with them. They will be his people, and God himself will be with them and be their God. He will wipe every tear from their eyes. There will be no more death or mourning or crying or pain, for the old order of things has passed away.' He who was seated on the throne said, 'I am making everything new!' Then he said, 'Write this down, for these words are trustworthy and true'"* (Revelation 21:3-5).

How do we begin to live like this now? We live in a daily declaration of dependence on the Holy Spirit. We take off the fleshly attitudes that we hide behind, and put on new ones. Paul put it this way in Colossians 3:8-10, *"But now you must also rid yourselves of all such things as these: anger, rage, malice, slander, and filthy language from your lips. Do not lie to each other, since you have taken off your old self with its practices and have put on the new self, which is being renewed in knowledge in the image of its Creator."*

We strip off the clothes of our old self, and put on the new wardrobe of who we are in Christ. It's then, and only then, we can be the right kind of naked.

LIFE APPLICATION

Are you authentic and open with others? Or are you playing a role to impress? Prayerfully spend some time considering whether you've consciously or unconsciously dressed up your real self to give others the impression that you're better than you really are.

OUR

SINS SEPARATE US FROM GOD

For all have sinned and
fall short of the glory of God.

- Romans 3:23

07 THE DEVIL'S DUE

Now the serpent was more crafty than any of the wild animals the LORD God had made. He said to the woman, "Did God really say, 'You must not eat from any tree in the garden? '" Genesis 3:1

You were anointed as a guardian cherub,
    for so I ordained you.
You were on the holy mount of God;
    you walked among the fiery stones.
You were blameless in your ways
    from the day you were created
    till wickedness was found in you.
Through your widespread trade
    you were filled with violence,
    and you sinned.
So I drove you in disgrace from the mount of God,
    and I expelled you, guardian cherub,
    from among the fiery stones.
Your heart became proud
    on account of your beauty,
and you corrupted your wisdom
    because of your splendor.
So I threw you to the earth;
    I made a spectacle of you before kings. Ezekiel 28:14-17

I'll never forget the first time I watched the previews to the 1973 horror film classic, *The Exorcist*. This film was groundbreaking for its time, and very graphic. It told the story of a twelve-year-old girl, who for some inexplicable reason, becomes possessed by the Devil. Her bed shakes, her body levitates and she vomits pea-green puke all over a holy water-flinging priest.

As soon as I watched the previews (which terrified me), my mom said, "Go to bed." I begged her to let me stay up a little while longer, but she made me go upstairs to my bedroom. I lay in my bed, almost sure I could feel it shaking. I began to cry out to my mom. Finally, she screamed up the stairs, "If you don't stay quiet, I'm gonna come up there and spank you!!!" I yelled back, "Please do!!!!" I figured a good old fashioned spanking was better than fighting off the Devil.

And that's the problem with many Christians. We tend to view the Devil more through the eyes of the producer of *The Exorcist*, than we do through the lens of Scripture.

According to the Bible, Satan started out as the anointed cherub, the guardian of the throne of God and the lead singer of the heavenly choir. He was beautiful, winsome and powerful. But pride filld his heart, and he rebelled against God and was cast out of heaven.

The Devil didn't suddenly grow horns and a tail.

But when he was cast out, he didn't suddenly turn ugly and grow horns and a tail. He is still beautiful. As 2 Corinthians 11:14 reminds us, *"...Satan himself masquerades as an angel of light."*

It was this angelic being who disguised himself as a serpent in the Garden of Eden, and tempted Eve. Perhaps serpents were much more much more beautiful back then before the Fall...

But whatever the reason, Eve was not taken aback by this creature. Rather, she was intrigued by him.

Why did he tempt Eve? Because the Devil wanted what he was sure was his due. He had already led the charge in a failed attempt to conquer Jesus in heaven, so now it was time to conquer the earth. And in many ways, when that bite-riddled piece of fruit hit the ground, he'd accomplished his goal.

The earth became the Devil's playground, and every baby born after that, except for Jesus Himself, would be born under his domain.

While Satan deceived Eve (1 Timothy 2:14), Adam knew exactly what he was doing when he took the forbidden fruit his wife offered him. He was choosing Satan's way over God's. Weeds took over—both in Eden, and in the hearts of humans ever since.

He's still whispering lies as an angel of light.

And it all started with a fallen power angel named Lucifer who wanted to hijack what God had given to Adam. The story of human history is told in this unfolding chess match between God and Satan in the battle for the hearts of humanity. While we know that God has held the final "checkmate" move since the beginning of time, in His sovereignty He is letting the chess match unfold to demonstrate His glorious wisdom and power.

But the Devil wants his due. He wants his due on the earth, and he wants his due in your heart. He's still whispering lies as an angel of light, hoping to lure you away from the true Light of the World—Jesus.

Don't listen to him. And, if you can, avoid pea-green soup.

LIFE APPLICATION

What lie is Satan trying to slither into your mind to mess up your relationship with God or with others? Maybe he's telling you...

"Your life has no purpose or meaning..."
"There's a reason nobody likes you. You're unlovable..."
"You're a loser. God can't use you..."

Label the lie. Invite God, through the Holy Spirit, to replace that lie with His truth.

You have purpose! Acts 26:16: *Now get to your feet. I have appeared to you to appoint you as a servant and as a witness of what you have seen and what you will see of me.*

You are loved! 1 John 4:10: *This is love: not that we loved God, but that he loved us and sent his Son as an atoning sacrifice for our sins.*

God can use you! 1 Corinthians 1:27: *But God chose the foolish things of the world to shame the wise; God chose the weak things of the world to shame the strong.*

Whatever deception you've fallen for in the Evil One's bag of lies, ask God to help you walk in the truth of James 4:7 in this area of your life: *"Submit yourselves, then, to God. Resist the devil and he will flee from you."*

THE ONE THING THAT RUINED EVERYTHING

Now the serpent was more crafty than any of the wild animals the LORD God had made. He said to the woman, "Did God really say, 'You must not eat from any tree in the garden'?"

The woman said to the serpent, "We may eat fruit from the trees in the garden, but God did say, 'You must not eat fruit from the tree that is in the middle of the garden, and you must not touch it, or you will die.'"

"You will not certainly die," the serpent said to the woman. "For God knows that when you eat from it your eyes will be opened, and you will be like God, knowing good and evil."

When the woman saw that the fruit of the tree was good for food and pleasing to the eye, and also desirable for gaining wisdom, she took some and ate it. She also gave some to her husband, who was with her, and he ate it. Genesis 3:1-6

Imagine it's hot outside and you've been doing yard work all day. I walk up to you with a cold glass of crystal clear water, and offer it to you. Without thinking or blinking, you smile and say "Yes." But before I extend the water to you, I take out a tablespoon full of a certain clear substance and pour it into the glass of water. You ask, "What is it?" I don't want to answer, but you insist. Finally I say, "It's just one little tablespoon of arsenic." And with that, I extend the cold glass of poison-laced water to you.

Would you drink it? Of course not!

It only takes one tablespoon of arsenic to kill an adult. If you drank it you would die.

In a spiritual sense, something similar happened when Adam took a bite of the forbidden fruit. That one "little" sin brought spiritual death and instantly injected depravity into the inborn nature of all humanity. From that moment on, things would never be the same. One little tablespoon of sin poisoned everything.

That's why you don't have to teach toddlers how to be selfish. It comes naturally. That's why we don't have to teach children how to misbehave. We have to show them how to be kind and generous.

One little tablespoon of sin poisoned everything.

But as we grow up, even our good acts become a cover up. They erupt from a desire to be perceived in a positive light by others, or to feel good about ourselves. In the words of spoken word artist Propaganda, "Even our good deeds are an extension of our selfishness."

Romans 5:12 puts it this way, *"Therefore, just as sin entered the world through one man, and death through sin, and in this way death came to all people, because all sinned."* Think of it this way, in Adam were all the seeds of all humanity. From his children would come more children, and from their children would come more children, from the beginning of time until the end of it. When Adam was corrupted, then so were his seeds. These seeds, once planted into the lineage of all humanity through the act of conception, brought physical life mixed with spiritual death.

That's why God warned Adam in Genesis 2:16-17, *"The LORD God commanded the man, 'You are free to eat from any tree in the garden, but you must not eat from the tree of the knowledge of good and evil, for when you eat from it you will surely die.'"*

The day that Adam ate the forbidden fruit, he didn't physically die—though that came later. But he did spiritually die—immediately. And in a sense, on that day, so did we. Through his willful choice to break God's commandment, Adam insured that deep down inside, we all start out as self-centered little hedonistic narcissists.

So don't be surprised when a child is selfish, and don't be shocked when someone cuts you off or flips you off in traffic. As a matter of fact, don't be surprised when you're selfish yourself. The depravity gene is in our DNA. No, it's not the new you in Jesus, but it's the old you that you still cart around in your flesh.

The depravity gene is in our DNA.

The Apostle Paul describes this ongoing battle we must wage with sin in Romans 7:21-25, *"So I find this law at work: Although I want to do good, evil is right there with me. For in my inner being I delight in God's law; but I see another law at work in me, waging war against the law of my mind and making me a prisoner of the law of sin at work within me. What a wretched man I am! Who will rescue me from this body that is subject to death? Thanks be to God, who delivers me through Jesus Christ our Lord!"*

Only Jesus can deliver us from the depravity at work in this world and in our flesh. He is the key to "re-Adamizing" Adam, and repairing the soul poison that's been passed on to us spiritually.

LIFE APPLICATION

Sometimes we seem surprised by the fact that the non-believers in our lives are making sinful choices. But the reality is that sinners sin; and so do we. It's in our nature. Picketing and politics won't change that. Only Jesus can change a heart from selfish to selfless. Ask God to soften your heart toward those who don't know Him personally. Watch your attitude during the next 24 hours, and when you're tempted to be critical—even if you feel you're totally justified in being critical—instead, be gracious and grace-giving.

09 DUCK AND COVER, HIDE AND BLAME

Then the eyes of both of them were opened, and they realized they were naked; so they sewed fig leaves together and made coverings for themselves.

Then the man and his wife heard the sound of the LORD God as he was walking in the garden in the cool of the day, and they hid from the LORD God among the trees of the garden. But the LORD God called to the man, "Where are you?"

He answered, "I heard you in the garden, and I was afraid because I was naked; so I hid."

And he said, "Who told you that you were naked? Have you eaten from the tree that I commanded you not to eat from?"

The man said, "The woman you put here with me-she gave me some fruit from the tree, and I ate it."

Then the Lord God said to the woman, "What is this you have done?"

The woman said, "The serpent deceived me, and I ate." Genesis 3:7-13

Therefore, just as sin entered the world through one man, and death through sin, and in this way death came to all people, because all sinned. Romans 5:12

What was Adam and Eve's first reaction after they disobeyed God?

To cover their shame!

Their sinful disobedience destroyed their innocence and opened their spiritual eyes. Their guilty consciences stirred, even before God came looking for them. Their disobedience triggered the very first shame and blame game. To this day, "fig leaves" are a euphemism for attempting to cover up something embarrassing or shameful.

What was their second reaction? To hide from God!

Have you ever tried to play a game of hide-and-seek with a toddler? They "hide" right out in the open, plainly visible, by simply covering their eyes with their hands. You see, toddlers think that if they can't see you, then you can't see them. Sort of sounds like Adam and Eve's attempt to hide from God, doesn't it?

God has never stopped calling out "Where are you?"

Of course, they couldn't actually hide from God…but they tried, nevertheless. And we humans have been playing a cosmic game of hide-and-seek ever since. One where God searches for us, but we futilely try to hide in the gardens of materialism, religion, philosophy, self-justification, or whatever. Yet God has never stopped calling out "Where are you?" to our lost and broken world.

Adam and Eve's third reaction? To play the blame game!

The finger pointing began almost immediately. Adam blamed Eve—and even, indirectly, attempted to blame God with his whiny excuse, *"The woman **you put here with me**—she gave me some fruit from the tree, and I ate it."* And when God turned His questioning gaze on Eve, what did she do? She blamed the serpent.

From this inauspicious beginning, all the way down through the millennia, we humans continue to use the blame game to cover our "mistakes." From marital fights to congressional finger pointing, from ethnic cleansing to diplomatic posturing, we've made an art form out of pushing the blame onto someone else.

But Romans 5:12 makes it clear that sin isn't just Adam and Eve's problem. It's our problem too. *"Therefore, just as sin entered the world through one man, and death through sin, and in this way death came to all people, because all sinned."*

Adam was humankind's spiritual representative before God. When he sinned, he sinned on our behalf. When Adam declared war on God through his singular act of rebellion, he was acting as our representative. As a result, whether we like it or not, the reality is that all of us declared war on God, as well. We see it in the distressing headlines in the news, and we sense it in the quiet chambers of our own hearts when we are tempted to lie or lust or envy.

We work hard not to let our sin show.

Adam's defiance of God opened the floodgates of sin, and corrupted our spiritual genome. The ugly truth is that Adam's sin nature spread like a genetic defect to every human down through the generations, including you and me.

From our vantage point, Adam and Eve's defensive maneuvers to "duck and cover, hide and blame," might look pitifully inept, until we examine our own defensive strategies with God and others when it comes to "sin management." We're just as guilty.

How about you? Have you ever experienced God calling you out in the cool of the evening? Have you felt that uncomfortable conviction of the Holy Spirit in your life?

Maybe you've responded defensively with a lame excuse like…

> "Here, I'll just do this little random act of kindness to make up for that bad thing I did earlier. It really wasn't so *terribly* bad. At least I'm not like so-and-so whose sin is so…"

> "No way, God, don't ask me to do *that.* I'd really rather just sit this one out, if it's all the same to you. That's just too far outside my comfort zone…"

> "That blowup today really wasn't my fault, God. If You'd only do something about that other person's problem with anger/jealousy/lying…"

And while we sometimes direct these lame excuses toward God, we also frequently use them to self-justify our feeble attempts at sin management. We work hard not to let our sin show—not really caring that much about our holy and pure God. Instead, we're frankly more concerned about what others would think of us if they only knew, rather than being focused on God's holy standard.

If we can manage to hide our sin well, then it's really not so bad, we tell ourselves. Or if it's one of those more socially acceptable sins, like the "relatively harmless" bad habit of gossip, or the culturally acceptable greed of materialism, no big deal. After all, everyone does those kinds of things.

We're not an axe murderer, after all.

LIFE APPLICATION

Duck and cover, hide and blame. We all do it. Ask yourself these three questions:

- When it comes to your sin do you care more about God's holy standard or about what others would think of you if "they only knew"?
- Is there a particular area of your life that comes to mind as you consider whether or not you're guilty of trying to sweep your own sin under the proverbial rug or blame others?
- What are you going to do about your answers to the two questions above?

Be honest before God, acknowledge your sin. Receive God's forgiveness and make changes.

No more duck and cover, hide and blame.

10 WHY LABOR PAINS, MARITAL FIGHTS AND WORK ARE A PAIN IN THE REAR

To the woman he said,

> *"I will make your pains in childbearing very severe;*
> *with painful labor you will give birth to children.*
> *Your desire will be for your husband,*
> *and he will rule over you."*

To Adam he said, "Because you listened to your wife and ate fruit from the tree about which I commanded you, 'You must not eat from it,'

> *"Cursed is the ground because of you;*
> *through painful toil you will eat food from it*
> *all the days of your life.*
> *It will produce thorns and thistles for you,*
> *and you will eat the plants of the field.*
> *By the sweat of your brow*
> *you will eat your food*
> *until you return to the ground,*
> *since from it you were taken;*
> *for dust you are*
> *and to dust you will return." Genesis 3:16-19*

Have you ever been sent to the principal's office? I have. I'll never forget going to Mrs. Wiebe's office when I was in seventh grade. While I've forgotten what I did wrong, I haven't forgotten how my heart pounded in my chest as I walked to her office, and waited for her to see me. Once I was ushered into her presence, she gave me a verbal scolding and then two spankings with a large, heavy, flat board. I remember being surprised by how much it hurt. Although I didn't cry (so punch my man card), I did let out a loud "OUCH!" Because it really did sting! Both the anticipation and the punishment were extremely uncomfortable.

Perhaps that's how Adam and Eve felt as they heard God walking around in the Garden looking for them. Imagine their beating hearts and their sweaty palms. Imagine that new and frightening sense of fear flooding their hearts, as they anticipated God's disappointment and punishment. And in their case, the punishment was far worse than the anticipation.

The first consequence doled out by a broken-hearted God was to the woman. Her punishment was pain in childbirth. I guess that if Adam and Eve had never sinned, somehow having babies would not be painful at all. But because of the Fall, hell hath no fury like a screaming, non-drugged mother, pushing out a small human. It's enough to make a church-going lady curse like a sailor.

Imagine that new, frightening sense of fear flooding their hearts.

The second consequence of the Fall was that wedding bliss would turn into a battleground. God tells Eve that *"Your desire will be for your husband, and he will rule over you."* The idea here is that the woman's desire would be to dominate her husband, and the husband's proclivity would be to rule like a dictator over his wife…therefore bringing friction to the bedrock relationship that should make society work.

Welcome to marriage, the battle royale, the rumble in the jungle. And it all started, not in a jungle, but in a garden.

Almost twenty years ago, back when I was a young, relatively newly married pastor, my wife and I were struggling. I was gone a lot of weekends and evenings. When I did come home, I was usually exhausted. She wanted to talk. I wanted to watch TV and tune out.

One night on the way to a Bible study, we got in a huge argument. (I'm sure that's never happened to you.) We fought a lot, but this one was especially intense. Sitting in the car in front of the house where the Bible study was, I told her to put on a happy face, because we had to go in.

Once in, Pastor Green, one of the associate pastors at our church, changed the game plan. He said, "Let's go around the room and do a "Life Application" about our lives and struggles tonight." I was thinking, "Oh great."

When he got to me, I tried to fake it. But my wife couldn't take it anymore. Although usually sweet and kind, she blew up at me, and then I went off. We were sitting there arguing in front of the stunned Bible study. (I think some of those present may have thought it was some kind of staged skit.) Pastor Green then went off on me. He told me that it didn't matter how big the ministry got, if I wasn't a good husband, it was all for naught. I said something like, "Yeah, well, I'm gonna kick your butt anyway!" With that I charged across the room with my hand clenched in a fist, ready to punch him right in the face. I figured I had sinned anyway, so I might as well go the whole way.

But then, right in the middle of that room, God hit me, instead. I fell to the ground in a weeping mess, because I knew my wife was right, and Pastor Green was right, and I was wrong. That meltdown saved my ministry. And, more importantly, that meltdown saved my marriage.

Maybe your marriage is in trouble. Realize that the problems you are facing extend back to the Fall of man. And the same God who rescued humanity can rescue your marriage.

Before the Fall, work was a joy. Now it's a pain.

The final consequence of the Fall laid out in today's Bible passage was that work is, generally speaking, a pain in the rear. God told Adam, *"'Cursed is the ground because of you; through painful toil you will eat food from it all the days of your life. It will produce thorns and thistles for you, and you will eat the plants of the field. By the sweat of your brow you will eat your food until you return to the ground.'"*

Before the Fall, work was a joy. Now it's a pain. The thorns and weeds of delayed deadlines, backbiting co-workers and shrinking paychecks are just a few of the struggles we face working in a fallen world.

Thanks, Adam.

LIFE APPLICATION

Only in Christ can we find the strength we need to overcome the consequences of the Fall. Whether it's the pain of a struggling marriage, a shattered parent-child relationship, the stress or drudgery of work or some other challenge in your life, the sad reality is that we all live with the consequences of Adam and Eve's fateful choice to turn away from God. Still, God is a very present help in time of trouble.

Spend a few minutes mediating on Psalm 46:1: *"God is our refuge and strength, an ever-present help in trouble."* Cling to Him as your refuge and strength. Silently rest in His strong presence. Then ask God for opportunities in the next 24 hours to live out and pass along His hope and strength to others in the midst of their time of trouble.

11 EVICTED!

And the LORD God said, "The man has now become like one of us, knowing good and evil. He must not be allowed to reach out his hand and take also from the tree of life and eat, and live forever." So the Lord God banished him from the Garden of Eden to work the ground from which he had been taken. After he drove the man out, he placed on the east side of the Garden of Eden cherubim and a flaming sword flashing back and forth to guard the way to the tree of life. Genesis 3:22-24

If you've ever been around a group of legalistic Christians, you know how ugly it can get when humans set themselves up as judge and jury, and think they are the ultimate arbiters of "knowing good and evil." I lived in that world for a few years, and once I found my way out of it, I discovered that grace is the only antidote for the poison of legalism gone wild.

Judging and condemning—that's what eating from the tree of the knowledge of good and evil unleashed. The Fall unleashed an arrogant insistence that we humans know best, and a willful drive to wrest control of all things moral away from the rightful hand of God. We desire to determine right from wrong in our own eyes. And then, once we arrive at our own personal conclusions, we strive to impose them on everyone around us.

No wonder the world has been haunted by wars, murder and mayhem down through the millennia. Judge or be judged. Control or be controlled.

Just imagine if there were no hope of ever escaping this judging, controlling manmade prison. What if your fate were sealed and your only prospect was to spend all eternity in

Grace is the only antidote for the poison of legalism.

this perpetual cycle of bearing the judgment and condemnation of others and your own guilty conscience—and most importantly, God?

Which makes one particular verse in today's passage so intriguing—a verse that's often overlooked in this familiar story about the Fall: *"He* [man] *must not be allowed to reach out his hand and take also from the tree of life and eat, and live forever."* And then the story picks back up with the part we know so well: *"So the Lord God banished him from the Garden of Eden ..."*

This verse about barring us from access to *"the tree of life"* makes it sounds like being banished from the Garden was actually some sort of mysterious combination of God's judgment AND His mercy. If humans had also eaten from *"the tree of life,"* it would have sealed us forever and always in our spoiled and broken state. We would be hopelessly trapped for all eternity in our ugly, judging, condemning, guilty ways.

By banishing us and blocking our access to *"the tree of life,"* God kept the pathway to spiritual redemption open. By closing the gates of Eden and guarding them with His holy cherubim, the wheels were set in motion for redemption through the cross, in the course of due time. And the cross would it make it possible for us to escape our fallen condition and spend eternity in restored relationship with God.

LIFE APPLICATION

Our human tendencies to be judgmental and hypocritical are part of the curse of the Fall. Our propensity for these sins can only be battled back with the help of the Holy Spirit producing His fruit in our lives. Check out Galatians 5:22: *"But the fruit of the Spirit is love, joy, peace, forbearance, kindness, goodness, faithfulness."* These are the antithesis of a judging, condemning spirit.

In light of the fruit of the Spirit, do a character check and prayerfully ask God for His insight as you address the following questions.

Are you personally judgmental? Are you quick to act as judge and jury when someone behaves in ways your Christian faith identifies as sin? Remember Jesus' response to those whose lifestyle choices were contrary to the Law (the Samaritan woman in John 4 and the woman caught in adultery in John 8:1-11). Do you approach others in a way that communicates that you are "just one beggar showing another beggar where to find bread"?

Are you hypocritical? Do you hold others to a higher standard than the one you live by inside your own soul? If you're really brave, ask your friends—including your non-Christian friends—whether they think you are judgmental or hypocritical. (Caution: Don't ask if you aren't willing to hear the truth without getting defensive.)

12 THE DYE DON'T LIE!

And God spoke all these words:

"I am the Lord your God, who brought you out of Egypt, out of the land of slavery.

"You shall have no other gods before me.

"You shall not make for yourself an image in the form of anything in heaven above or on the earth beneath or in the waters below. You shall not bow down to them or worship them; for I, the Lord your God, am a jealous God, punishing the children for the sin of the parents to the third and fourth generation of those who hate me, but showing love to a thousand generations of those who love me and keep my commandments.

"You shall not misuse the name of the LORD your God, for the LORD will not hold anyone guiltless who misuses his name.

"Remember the Sabbath day by keeping it holy. Six days you shall labor and do all your work, but the seventh day is a sabbath to the LORD your God. On it you shall not do any work, neither you, nor your son or daughter, nor your male or female servant, nor your animals, nor any foreigner residing in your towns. For in six days the LORD made the heavens and the earth, the sea, and all that is in them, but he rested on the seventh day. Therefore the LORD blessed the Sabbath day and made it holy.

"Honor your father and your mother, so that you may live long in the land the LORD your God is giving you.

"You shall not murder.

"You shall not commit adultery.

"You shall not steal.

"You shall not give false testimony against your neighbor.

"You shall not covet your neighbor's house. You shall not covet your neighbor's wife, or his male or female servant, his ox or donkey, or anything that belongs to your neighbor."
Exodus 20:1-17

When God thundered out the Ten Commandments to Moses, our fate was sealed. These seemingly innocuous commandments are impossible to keep in a way that God deems acceptable.

With the Ten Commandments, our fate was sealed.

Ask the typical person who believes in some sort of God what it takes to get to heaven, and they'll likely say something like "be good" or "keep the Ten Commandments" or something similar. But what that person often doesn't realize is that the standard these Commandments hold us to is not just one of "trying to keep them," but one of actually keeping them all the time, without fail and with no selfish, ulterior motives.

For the Ten Commandments to "work," they must be obeyed consistently, comprehensively and carefully.

1. **They must be obeyed consistently (without fail!)** *"For all who rely on the works of the law are under a curse, as it is written: 'Cursed is everyone who does not continue to do everything written in the Book of the Law.'"* Galatians 3:10
    One slip up and you're cursed. Yes, that means if you dishonor your parents one time, or tell one "little white lie," then you are forever condemned. The only brand of righteousness that God accepts is 100% pure.

2.   **They must be obeyed comprehensively (without compromise!)** *"For whoever keeps the whole law and yet stumbles at just one point is guilty of breaking all of it."* James 2:10. Basically if you forget to honor the Sabbath one time, you might as well have broken every one of the Ten Commandments. When you break the law—any law—that makes you a lawbreaker.

3.   **They must be obeyed carefully (without selfishness!)** According to Francis Schaeffer in *True Spirituality*, "The climax of the Ten Commandments is the Tenth Commandment—'Thou shalt not covet'—this commandment is an entirely inward thing. Actually, we break this commandment before we break any of the others. Paul states very clearly in Romans [7:7-8] that this was the commandment which gave him a 'sense of being sinful'... What Paul is saying here is this: 'I did not know I was a sinner; I thought I would come out all right, because I was keeping these outward things and was doing well in comparison with other people.'" [4]

So even if it was possible to obey all the law all the time outwardly, if you've had one covetous internal motive, even once — like to look better than the other guy trying to keep the commandments—then it's all for naught.

I once went to the dentist to get some work done on my teeth. As usual, she asked me the inevitable question, "Have you been brushing and flossing?" I told her that I'd been brushing and flossing some. Then she said words that sent a shiver down my spine, "Well, we're about to find out. I'm going to put some blue dye on your teeth, and it will show whether or not you've been brushing and flossing. It will expose every area where you've not been taking good care of your teeth. And, Greg, the dye don't lie.

As she applied the dye to my teeth, turned on the light and made me look in the mirror and smile, I was horrified. There were blue stains everywhere, and I was caught red handed and blue teethed...a sinner in the hands of an angry dentist.

In a similar way, the law is like a dye that shows us how far we fall short. The dye couldn't clean my teeth, it just exposed my plaque. In the same way, the law can't cleanse us from our sin, but it clearly exposes it.

The law is like a dye that shows us how far we fall short.

LIFE APPLICATION

As God brings opportunities our way to share our faith and talk to people about the reality that "Our sins separate us from God," we must never hesitate to admit that we're sinners, too.

There's a simple approach to sharing your faith with others that naturally folds this truth into your conversation. It's called "Ask-Admire-Admit." Here's how it works:

ASK the person you're talking to questions about what they believe. Not to trap them, but to understand them, and break down any relational barriers that might keep them from considering Jesus.

ADMIRE everything you can about what they believe in order to help them open up. Find areas of common ground you can compliment them on. Even if you don't agree with their beliefs, you can always affirm their honesty.

ADMIT that the reason you are a Christian is that you know you've fallen short and need someone to rescue you. That someone is Jesus.

As you ask honest questions, admire what you can about what others believe and admit your own need for Jesus, their guard will drop and you can begin to engage them in a real conversation about the good news of the gospel.

You can watch a short video that explains more about how to use the "Ask-Admire-Admit" approach at dare2share.org/worldviews. And if you have friends who are coming from a particular religious or worldview, check out the faith sharing questions, compliments and insights you can find on that webpage for thirteen diverse, distinct worldviews.

Have an "Ask-Admire-Admit" conversation today with someone who doesn't know Jesus personally.

13 WOE IS ME!

In the year that King Uzziah died, I saw the Lord, high and exalted, seated on a throne; and the train of his robe filled the temple. Above him were seraphim, each with six wings: With two wings they covered their faces, with two they covered their feet, and with two they were flying. And they were calling to one another:

"Holy, holy, holy is the LORD Almighty;
    the whole earth is full of his glory."

At the sound of their voices the doorposts and thresholds shook and the temple was filled with smoke.

"Woe to me!" I cried. "I am ruined! For I am a man of unclean lips, and I live among a people of unclean lips, and my eyes have seen the King, the Lord Almighty."
Isaiah 6:1-5

One of the scariest movie characters from my childhood was the Wicked Witch of the West in *The Wizard of Oz*. She not only tormented poor Dorothy and her timid friends, she scared me witless. Perhaps that's why her demise is so indelibly imprinted in brain. Remember?

Just after the Wicked Witch sets the helpless scarecrow on fire, Dorothy grabs a bucket of water and throws it to put out the flames. Unbeknownst to everyone except the witch herself, water is her mortal downfall. She immediately begins her lament, crying, "I'm melting! I'm melting! Oh, my world, my world…I'm going, I'm going…"

In seconds, the Wicked Witch is totally undone by simply coming into contact with water. She quickly melts away into the floor.

We get some of that same feeling in today's passage from Isaiah. But instead of contact with water melting him away, it's contact with the holiness of God Almighty that sends him into a meltdown of a different sort. *"Woe to me!" he cries, "I am ruined!...my eyes have seen the King, the Lord Almighty."*

Contact with the holiness of God triggered a meltdown.

Isaiah's "Woe to me!" response is even more striking, if we look at it in light of the previous chapter in the book of Isaiah, which gives it some remarkable context.

As an Old Testament prophet of God, Isaiah is highly experienced when it comes to delivering messages of woe. In Isaiah 5, just one chapter earlier than his dramatic, personal vision of God's holiness, the prophet delivers a whole string of woeful curses on the sinful Hebrew nation. Six times in this single chapter, he pronounces prophetic doom upon the wicked, declaring *"Woe to those who..."*

> ...accumulate more and more possessions
> ...make their lives all about drinking and partying
> ...pursue wickedness and ignore God
> ...call evil good and good evil
> ...are clever in their own sight
> ...are unjust to the innocent.

But now in Isaiah 6, when the prophet is actually given a personal vision of God's holiness, it's no longer *"Woe to those..."* It's *"Woe is me!"*

Isaiah was instantly overcome by his own sinfulness, and sensed his very being might collapse beneath the weight of his sin's ugliness in the presence of God's pure holiness.

Notice that even the seraphim, God's heavenly creatures, covered their faces and feet, concealing themselves as much as possible from the direct presence of God, as they cried out *"Holy, Holy, Holy is the Lord Almighty."* God's heavenly holiness blazes so brightly that it appears both heavenly and earthly creatures are overcome in its presence.

This passage gives us a sobering look at why no human can ever enter into the presence of our holy, pure and perfect God through the power of their own human efforts to be "good enough." We are all sinful. We have all fallen short and missed the mark of God's holy perfection.

The chasm between us and our holy God is immensely vast. Trying to bridge that chasm ourselves is like trying to throw a rock at the moon. You'll never come even close through your own efforts. You may throw it farther than I can, or than anybody on this earth can, for that matter, but you still won't have a chance of actually hitting the moon. Why? Because the moon is 238,900 miles away from the earth. Even if you had the most amazing arm on earth and could throw a rock a mile high, you wouldn't even start coming close to hitting the moon.

The chasm between us and our holy God is immensely vast.

The same is true with measuring up to God's holy standards. We're not even close. You could be the nicest person on the planet, but you still miss the mark of God's holy standard by miles and miles.

LIFE APPLICATION

The awestruck chant *"Holy, holy, holy"* appears only one other place in Scripture. In Revelation 4, we find the writer once again describing how God's heavenly creatures gather around His Throne, continually repeating day and night:

> *"'Holy, holy, holy*
> *is the Lord God Almighty,'*
> *who was, and is, and is to come."* . . .

> *"You are worthy, our Lord and God,*
> *to receive glory and honor and power,*
> *for you created all things,*
> *and by your will they were created*
> *and have their being."* Revelation 4:8b, 11

Quiet your mind, close your eyes, calm your soul, enter His presence and meditate for a few minutes on the holiness of God. Let His holiness blow your mind, and scare you witless, for *"The fear of the Lord is the beginning of wisdom, and knowledge of the Holy One is understanding"* (Proverbs 9:10).

SINS

CANNOT BE DEEDS
REMOVED BY GOOD

All of us have become
like one who is unclean,
and all our righteous acts
are like filthy rags.

- Isaiah 64:6a

14 RAISING CAIN

Adam made love to his wife Eve, and she became pregnant and gave birth to Cain. She said, "With the help of the Lord I have brought forth a man." Later she gave birth to his brother Abel.

Now Abel kept flocks, and Cain worked the soil. In the course of time Cain brought some of the fruits of the soil as an offering to the LORD. And Abel also brought an offering-fat portions from some of the firstborn of his flock. The LORD looked with favor on Abel and his offering, but on Cain and his offering he did not look with favor. So Cain was very angry, and his face was downcast.

Then the LORD said to Cain, "Why are you angry? Why is your face downcast? If you do what is right, will you not be accepted? But if you do not do what is right, sin is crouching at your door; it desires to have you, but you must rule over it."

Now Cain said to his brother Abel, "Let's go out to the field." While they were in the field, Cain attacked his brother Abel and killed him.

Then the LORD said to Cain, "Where is your brother Abel?"

"I don't know," he replied. "Am I my brother's keeper?"

The Lord said, "What have you done? Listen! Your brother's blood cries out to me from the ground. Now you are under a curse and driven from the ground, which opened its mouth to receive your brother's blood from your hand. Genesis 4:1-11

From square one, we see fallen humanity trying to justify itself before a holy God. It started with Adam blaming Eve, and continued with Cain offering veggies to God, instead of an animal sacrifice like his little brother Abel.

Is offering a basket full of vegetables verses a bowl full of lamb's blood really that big of a deal? To God it is!

Because the basket represented something God rejects, while the bowl represented something God accepts. The basket of vegetables represented all Cain's human efforts that he was offering to God, for he'd worked hard to produce them through the sweat of his brow. If you've ever worked a garden, you'll understand exactly what I'm saying.

The basket represented something God rejects.

Years ago, when my wife and I bought our first house, a small 900 square foot, three bedroom hut, it came with a 935 square foot unkempt garden…plus chickens.

My wife was dead set on reviving the garden, and asked me to join her. I reluctantly agreed, and set about to revitalize this dead piece of land. One of the first things I did was scrape loose and shovel out the four or five inches of chicken dung caking the bottom of the chicken pens. Wheel barrowing it out to the garden, I tilled it into the soil. There must have been 20 wheel barrows full of chicken dung.

And let me tell you something, chicken poop is like steroids for gardens. We produced over 500 tomatoes that year, along with loads of other vegetables. We were proud of our "little" garden, and as we handed bag after bag full of rich sweet tomatoes out to our grateful neighbors, we had that satisfying sense of "yup, we produced that."

One German neighbor, in particular, swore up and down that the ground in our part of town was unfruitful. When I showed him our garden, he freaked out, and I swelled up with pride.

"What must we do to do the works God requires?"

It was that same brand of chest-popping arrogance that Cain felt when he offered his basket full of veggies to God. He had planted, cultivated and harvested them. Here was the fruit of his efforts.

But God rejected his offering. Why? The same reason God rejects any human attempt to pacify his anger toward sin through hard work and self effort! Because all of these attempts are rooted in pride, not humility.

Abel, on the other hand, just took a lamb from his flock, and sacrificed it. He knew that God required a blood sacrifice. He knew that something innocent must die for his sins. And he knew that he had nothing to do with his own salvation. As a result, *"The LORD looked with favor on Abel and his offering, but on Cain and his offering he did not look with favor."*

Cain got mad. Cain killed Abel.

And we've been "raising Cain" ever since. Cain was raised in Naaman's heart when he was told to dip himself in the Jordan seven times to rid himself of leprosy. He wanted to do something *himself* to get rid of the leprosy, but instead he had to humble himself and go under the muddy waters of the Jordon seven times.

Cain was raised in Saul's heart when he took matters into his own hands, instead of waiting for the Prophet Samuel to arrive.

Cain was raised in the Pharisees' hearts in John 6:28-29, when they heard Jesus' response to the question, *"What must we do to do the works God requires?"* For Jesus simply said, *"The work of God is this: to believe in the one he has sent."*

Cain was raised in Jewish hearts when Paul preached the gospel that welcomed the Gentiles freely into the family of God by faith and faith alone.

When we try to please God by what we do, then we are "raising Cain." But when we please God by trusting in His Son, then we are following the example of Cain's right-hearted little brother.

LIFE APPLICATION

Consider these questions:

- What are your primary motivations when you do something "good"? Are you trying to earn God's good opinion, so He'll bless you and make your life pleasant and prosperous? Or are you seeking to serve Him out of gratitude for His gift of grace?
- Do you sometimes find yourself drifting into the mindset that God got a pretty good deal when He got you?

15 FILTHY RAGS

All of us have become like one who is unclean,
*   and all our righteous acts are like filthy rags;*
we all shrivel up like a leaf,
*   and like the wind our sins sweep us away.* Isaiah 64:6

As I mentioned earlier, I used to be a roofer. In general, it's safe to say that roofing is a hot, sweaty, demanding job—one you definitely want to clean up from after a hard day's work. But there's one particular roofing crew assignment that beats all the others when it comes to getting dirty. It's called being the "kettle guy." That's what we called the person who was assigned to work the tar kettle when we were putting on an asphalt roof. The kettle guy would melt down 100 pound kegs of tar in a kettle. Tar would get on everything, especially the person manning the kettle. When I was the "kettle guy," I would leave work at the end of the day covered in tar and grime.

During this time that I was working as a roofer, I was dating Debbie, the girl who would later become my wife. So every time I had a date with Debbie, I wouldn't dream of going out with her while I was filthy with the tar and grime from my day's work. I wanted to put my best foot forward, so I rubbed and scrubbed to get cleaned up before I presented myself to her.

Sometimes I think we try to take that same sort of approach with God. We think we can scrub off the filth of our bad deeds with our good deeds. The problem is that with God, even our good deeds come up short. Which is why Isaiah says, *"all our righteous acts are like filthy rags."*

Have you ever done something nice for someone and then given yourself a mental pat on the back for your good deed? Maybe you've even found your thoughts drifting in a direction that goes something like one of these...

- "Well, that should make God happy with me..."
- "I'm glad I did that. It makes me feel good about myself..."
- "I'll bet that impressed them! Now they know what a nice person I am..."
- "Well, I've done my good deed for the day...check that off my list...maybe now God will get me that parking spot I need..."

Those kinds of thoughts have one thing in common: a self-righteous attitude. They give us a glimpse into how even our "righteous acts" are birthed out of mixed motives and self-righteousness. Because even our "good deeds" are tainted by an inner core of selfishness that bleeds into everything we think, say and do. Something deep down inside us twists everything we do (apart from Christ). Our ego seeps into every corner of who we are and what we do, so that compared against the standards of our holy, pure and perfect God, our BEST efforts measure up to nothing more than filthy rags.

Do you really believe that your inherent sinful nature makes you "unclean" before God? Isaiah's metaphor of being like one who is "unclean" is largely lost on us today. But back in his time, "unclean" carried a shockingly vivid meaning, for it drew upon the Old Testament law. The great preacher Charles Spurgeon unpacked the metaphor for his congregation by explaining that under Jewish law, "when a person was unclean he could not go up to the house of the Lord. He could offer no sacrifice. God could accept nothing at his hands; he was an outcast and an alien so long as he remained unclean."[5]

And that's the picture being painted here for us spiritually. We are outcasts and aliens in God's kingdom. We have absolutely no grounds to approach God and enter into a personal relationship with Him on the basis of our own efforts. Ephesians 2:8-9 clearly and succinctly shows us the futility of thinking our own righteous acts will help us earn our back to God: *"For it is by grace you have been saved, through faith-and this is not from yourselves, it is the gift of God-not by works, so that no one can boast."* It's only because of the work Christ did on the cross that God washes us clean and embraces us with open arms.

LIFE APPLICATION

Have a conversation with God about the following Bible verses.

"No," said Peter, *"you shall never wash my feet."* Jesus answered, *"Unless I wash you, you have no part with me"* (John 13:8).

"Cleanse me with hyssop, and I will be clean; wash me, and I will be whiter than snow" (Psalm 51:7).

As you go through your day, every time you wash your hands, think about your conversation with God and about being washed clean by Jesus.

16 THE SCARIEST SERMON EVER PREACHED

"You have heard that it was said to the people long ago, 'You shall not murder, and anyone who murders will be subject to judgment.' But I tell you that anyone who is angry with a brother or sister will be subject to judgment..."

"...You have heard that it was said, 'You shall not commit adultery.' But I tell you that anyone who looks at a woman lustfully has already committed adultery with her in his heart.

"If your right eye causes you to stumble, gouge it out and throw it away. It is better for you to lose one part of your body than for your whole body to be thrown into hell. And if your right hand causes you to stumble, cut it off and throw it away. It is better for you to lose one part of your body than for your whole body to go into hell..."

"...You have heard that it was said, 'Love your neighbor and hate your enemy.' But I tell you, love your enemies and pray for those who persecute you..."

"...Be perfect, therefore, as your heavenly Father is perfect." Matthew 5:21-22; 27-30; 43-44; 48

It's uncomfortable for me to listen to preachers who think that the Sermon on the Mount is some feel good, pull yourself up by your own bootstraps sermon. No, it is the most beautifully-worded, horrific sermon every preached. Those who heard it must have been thinking, "Holy crud! I'm going straight to hell."

Far scarier than Jonathan Edwards' "Sinners in the Hands of an Angry God" sermon, these words of Jesus go straight for the jugular, and illuminate our utter depravity with the white hot glare of God's holiness. Listening to this sermon was like staring into the sun, spiritually speaking. Because staring into the Son that day, would have provided a retina-burning view of the stark reality that you were a sinner on the highway to hell—no ifs, ands or buts about it.

Here's my paraphrase of what Jesus was basically saying…

"If you've ever lusted, you're an adulterer.

"If you've ever hated, you're a murderer.

"If you don't love your enemy, you're a sinner.

"If you're not as good as God, then you're going to hell."

It's the most beautifully-worded, horrific sermon every preached.

In just one short sermon, Jesus illuminates the law fully, and our depravity completely. Going beyond the words on the pages of the Torah, he brings to light the Ten Commandments' meaning, their full intent and the ultimate consequences of failing to keep them perfectly.

Personally, it was this very reality that prepared me to hear the gospel. When I was just a kid, I had heard some preacher or Sunday school teacher say that I had to confess my sins to be saved. I thought if I missed one, I would be going straight to hell. So I would confess all the sins that an eight-year-old could remember. Once I was done, I would mentally utter a curse word. Then, I'd confess that. Then, I'd drop the F-bomb in my brain. Then, I'd confess that. I was sure that if I died between the curse word and the confession, I'd be going straight to hell.

But God used the frustration and conviction that the law stirred up in my soul to prepare me for the message of grace. The guilt trip I was on packed my bags for the grace trip Jesus wanted to take me on.

Just two days ago, I was talking to a young Muslim named Mohammed in a Starbucks. After talking with him for a bit, I shared with him about how much God loved him. The very thought that God would love even him stunned this young man. He responded to me by explaining that Allah would only love him if he was good. So I asked him if he thought he was a good person. He said yes. So I took him to the words of Jesus in Matthew 5 about the price of admission into heaven, if he wanted to get there through the law door. The more I explained that God looks at our internal thoughts and motives, and not just our external actions, the more nervous he got.

The Sermon on the Mount pushes us off the cliff.

Then I shared with him the good news of what Jesus did for him on the cross 2,000 years ago. While Mohammed didn't trust in Jesus that day, my prayer is that the frustration and conviction of the law that drove me to my knees in simple faith in Christ's finished work, will do the same for this Muslim man.

The Sermon on the Mount pushes us off the cliff. But it's only so we know that we need to be rescued.

LIFE APPLICATION

Many Christians struggle under the heavy weight of the high standards set out in the Sermon on the Mount. Does that describe you? If so, I encourage you to take your burden to God, and have a conversation with Him about Matthew 11:28-30:

> *"Come to me, all you who are weary and burdened, and I will give you rest. Take my yoke upon you and learn from me, for I am gentle and humble in heart, and you will find rest for your souls. For my yoke is easy and my burden is light."*

And just like I had the chance to share the gospel with this young Muslim at Starbucks, you never know when God will drop an opportunity in your lap to strike up a spiritual conversation. Are you prepared to share the message of Jesus' love and grace with others—be they friends or strangers?

For help with this, I encourage you to download the Dare 2 Share faith-sharing mobile app. The "Share Now" section of the app will provide you with a quick and simple way to share the gospel using the six words of the GOSPEL acrostic.

17 WILL THE RICH YOUNG RULER BE IN HEAVEN?

As Jesus started on his way, a man ran up to him and fell on his knees before him. "Good teacher," he asked, "what must I do to inherit eternal life?"

"Why do you call me good?" Jesus answered. "No one is good—except God alone. You know the commandments: 'You shall not murder, you shall not commit adultery, you shall not steal, you shall not give false testimony, you shall not defraud, honor your father and mother.'"

"Teacher," he declared, "all these I have kept since I was a boy."

Jesus looked at him and loved him. "One thing you lack," he said. "Go, sell everything you have and give to the poor, and you will have treasure in heaven. Then come, follow me."

At this the man's face fell. He went away sad, because he had great wealth. Mark 10:17-22

There are certain passages that make us squirm, and this passage is one of them. You can't read the words of Jesus in these verses without thinking, "Have I given up enough?" "Should I sell everything and give it to the poor?" "What does it really take to be saved?" We often leave this passage, like the rich young ruler…saddened, grieving and scratching our heads.

But was Jesus really saying that to get to heaven we have to keep the Ten Commandments and give all our stuff to the poor to be saved? Now, I know you may be tempted to qualify this passage by thinking, "Well, no, but you have to be willing to do all of that." But a mere "willingness" to give it all up, robs this passage of its power. Jesus is asking the rich young ruler for more than willingness, he's asking him for everything.

If we're honest, in the deepest parts of our hearts, we know that we fall way short in the same way the rich young ruler did. We, like him, have broken the law, and according to Jesus in Matthew 5:21-30, continue to break it every time we lust or hate. We all have something we've not given up—food, shelter, time, iPad, and so on. We all fall short, when it comes to following Jesus. Not only do we fall short, we fall grossly short. Maybe that's why Paul, empowered by the Spirit of Jesus, wrote the inspired words, *"For all have sinned and fall short of the glory of God"* (Romans 3:23).

He was spiritually bankrupt before a holy God.

I'm convinced that when Jesus was talking to the rich young ruler, He was not painting a clear picture of the gospel. No, He was painting a clear picture of the law, and the law's true requirements. In one brilliant stroke, Jesus helped this young man—who initially thought he was a pretty good person—to see the covetousness, greed and narcissism that ruled his darkened heart. Maybe in this instant, the rich young ruler first understood that he was spiritually bankrupt before a holy God. Perhaps for the very first time, he experienced a genuine and sobering conviction of sin.

It's interesting to me that Mark 10:21 tells us, *"Jesus looked at him and loved him."* Jesus so deeply loved this young man, He had to break him of his self-dependency, and expose him for the sinner that he was. He had to show him that, if he wanted to earn eternal life by keeping the law, he had to go the whole way. It would take continual, total obedience and full surrender to every command, for all of his life. Jesus had to show him the impossibility of trying to earn this brand of righteousness before God. Because it is only once people are convinced that they're sinners, that they know they need a Savior.

In Romans 3:19-20, the Apostle Paul wrote, *"Now we know that whatever the law says, it says to those who are under the law, so that every mouth may be silenced and the whole world held accountable to God. Therefore no one will be declared righteous in God's sight by the works of the law; rather, through the law we become conscious of our sin."*

Jesus used the letter and spirit of the Ten Commandments to help this ruler come to "the knowledge of sin" in his own life. The spotlight of the law showcased the utter depravity inside his soul.

It's only when a person understands that they are lost, that they can be found. Jesus showed this young man that he was lost.

I sometimes wonder if in the frustrating years that followed this encounter with Jesus, whether or not God dispatched one of His followers to share the message of grace with this young man whom He loved. I imagine a Christ follower sharing that this same Jesus who exposed the ruler's sin so long ago, exposed His own back to the whip, His head to a crown of thorns and His soul to God when He screamed, *"My God! My God! Why have you forsaken me?"* All because He loved him. This same Judge who showed him how sinful he was, died in his place on the cross, so that through simple faith, he could be saved.

We'll never be able to sell or surrender enough.

Those who use this passage to preach a "you-better-give-up-everything-to-be-saved" type sermon, may be missing the deeper message of Jesus. Because, apart from Christ's death payment on the cross, we'll never be able to measure up to His standard of righteousness. We'll never be able to give up enough, sell enough or surrender enough…and that's the point.

That's the point of the law, and that's the point of this encounter.

And once a person realizes that they're a sinner in need of a Savior, they're finally ready to embrace the free gift of God's grace through faith in Jesus as their only hope of salvation.

Will we see the rich young ruler in heaven? I don't know, but if I were a betting man, I'd say yes. If Jesus loved this young man enough to take the time to expose his sin, then it seems like Jesus would love him enough to send someone down the line to share His message of grace through faith alone, in Christ alone.

LIFE APPLICATION

Jesus felt love in His heart for this young man, and demonstrated it in a piercing and powerful way. Do you know someone who thinks they are good enough to make it to heaven on their own merits? Maybe ask them to read the story of the rich young ruler in Mark 10:17-22, and ask them, based on this passage, how good a person has to be to get to heaven. Use it as an opportunity to share the real meaning of this passage, and introduce them to the grace of the Lord Jesus Christ.

Or acquire a copy of the outreach book *Life in 6 Words* available at store.dare2share. org, read it, then give it away.

18 THE PASTOR, THE BOY SCOUT AND THE SMARTEST MAN IN THE WORLD

To some who were confident of their own righteousness and looked down on everyone else, Jesus told this parable: "Two men went up to the temple to pray, one a Pharisee and the other a tax collector. The Pharisee stood by himself and prayed: 'God, I thank you that I am not like other people-robbers, evildoers, adulterers—or even like this tax collector. I fast twice a week and give a tenth of all I get.'

"But the tax collector stood at a distance. He would not even look up to heaven, but beat his breast and said, 'God, have mercy on me, a sinner.'

"I tell you that this man, rather than the other, went home justified before God. For all those who exalt themselves will be humbled, and those who humble themselves will be exalted." Luke 18:9-14

Have you heard the one about the pastor, the Boy Scout, and the brilliant Wall Street hedge fund manager who were flying together on a small plane?

In flight, the plane developed catastrophic mechanical trouble, so the pilot went to these three passengers and announced that the plane was going down. Unfortunately, he added, "There are only three parachutes, even though there are four of us on board. I should have one of the parachutes, because I have a wife and three small children." So he promptly took one and jumped.

The Wall Street analyst said, "I should get a parachute, because I'm one of the smartest men in the world, and the world needs me." So he took one and jumped.

The pastor and Boy Scout looked at each other. Then the pastor volunteered, "I know the Lord. I'm not afraid to die. You're young and have your whole life ahead of you. You take the remaining parachute, and I'll go down with the plane."

God is not impressed when we're impressed with ourselves.

The Boy Scout smiled and said, "No worries, Pastor, one of the smartest men in the world just put on my backpack and jumped out!"

The moral of the story? Pride goeth before the fall.

There's a sense in which Jesus is making a similar point in the parable He tells in Luke 18, for His punch line to the story is simple: *"For all those who exalt themselves will be humbled, and those who humble themselves will be exalted."*

God is not impressed when we're impressed with ourselves. He doesn't care about our outward façade of going through the motions of "being religious." He looks into our hearts.

Let's take a closer look at the respective prayers of these two contrasting characters.

The proud Pharisee…
- Looked at sinners with contempt, rather than compassion
- Drew attention to his outward acts of righteousness
- Compared himself to others, rather than to God's standard of pure holiness
- Was grateful only for his own accomplishments
- Failed to seek God's mercy. He was so busy being self-righteous that he failed to realize he needed it.

In contrast, the tax collector…

- Approached God humbly, not even daring to look up to heaven
- Knew he was a sinner
- Measured himself against the perfect standard of the law, not others
- Was distraught about his sin and truly repentant
- Was honest and authentic before God
- Genuinely sought God's mercy and grace.

Jesus' parable beautifully illustrates the sharp contrast between proud, puffed-up, religious folks who are confident they can earn their way to heaven through their own efforts, and the humble, repentant, sinner who realizes He desperately needs a Savior. Proud, pious, self-righteous posturing counts for nothing in God's economy. Sins cannot be removed by good deeds. They can only be removed by God's grace.

Whether you're a pastor, a Boy Scout, a nice little old lady who bakes pies for every church social or you just got out of prison for murder, all of us are just beggars together at the foot of the cross.

> ## We're all just beggars together at the foot of the cross.

We must all fall on God's mercy and grace, available through Jesus' atoning death and resurrection. It's our parachute. It's our only hope.

LIFE APPLICATION

Take another look at the bullet points that described the Pharisee's prayer. Do any of those attitudes characterize your spiritual life? Spend some time right now approaching God like the humble sinner in Jesus' story. Come before Him humbly, and genuinely seek His grace and mercy.

19 THE ULTIMATE REJECTION

"Not everyone who says to me, 'Lord, Lord,' will enter the kingdom of heaven, but only the one who does the will of my Father who is in heaven. Many will say to me on that day, 'Lord, Lord, did we not prophesy in your name and in your name drive out demons and in your name perform many miracles?' Then I will tell them plainly, 'I never knew you. Away from me, you evildoers!'" Matthew 7:21-23

One of my best friends, Dave Gibson, is a long-time missions pastor at Grace Church in Eden Prairie, Minnesota. He shares Jesus across his city and around the world with love, grace and truth. Dave has developed a little sermon outline with a big punch, based on Matthew 7:21-23.

These scary words of Jesus deal with the ultimate rejection. Now I've been rejected many times before. In high school, I was rejected by a girl I thought I was in love with—but I kept trying anyway! In college, I was rejected by a girl I *knew* I was in love with—but eventually married her!

But the ultimate rejection has nothing to do with dating, and everything to do with salvation. Jesus made this clear in His attention-getting proclamation, *"I never knew you. Away from me, you evildoers!"*

So who are these evildoers Jesus is talking about? Are they vile whoremongers? Let's dig a little deeper. The answer may surprise you.

1. They profess Christ, but don't possess Christ.

These people who are rejected and condemned to hell say a lot of the right things. They call Jesus who He actually is—*"Lord!"* They even say it twice, for emphasis. But it's not a matter of just saying the right words verbally.

It's not a matter of just saying the right words.

Paul put it this way in Romans 10:9-10, *"If you declare with your mouth, 'Jesus is Lord,' and believe in your heart that God raised him from the dead, you will be saved. For it is with your heart that you believe and are justified, and it is with your mouth that you profess your faith and are saved."*

According to these verses, it appears that there will be people in hell who said "The Sinner's Prayer" with their lips ("Lord! Lord!"), but never actually believed in their heart. It's not a matter of saying the right things. It's a matter of trusting in the right person, Jesus Himself!

2. They practice religion, with no personal relationship.

Jesus said, *"Many will say to me on that day, 'Lord, Lord, did we not prophesy in your name and in your name drive out demons and in your name perform many miracles?'"*

These religious people say the right things, and do the right things, but they don't believe in the right Person. They believe in themselves, their inherent goodness and their ability to razzle and dazzle with miracles and ministry. But God sees beyond the sizzle, to the maggot-riddled steak they're cooking.

Religion is no substitute for a relationship with God. The word "religion" comes from the Latin word which means "to bind back." It's man's attempt to bind himself back to

God through deeds and creeds. But the only thing that can bind back what has been broken is the grace of God, extended to us through Jesus Christ.

3. They will perish in hell, instead of enjoy paradise in heaven.

"Then I will tell them plainly, 'I never knew you. Away from me, you evildoers!'

Jesus calls them evildoers, not because of what they did, but because of why they did it, and because of who they were trusting in. They did the right things for the wrong reasons in order to make themselves feel and look good.

Religion is no substitute for a relationship with God.

As a result, they will be eternally condemned to an everlasting hell from which there is no escape. Paul reiterates this disturbing reality in 2 Thessalonians 1:8-9 when he says, *"He will punish those who do not know God and do not obey the gospel of our Lord Jesus. They will be punished with everlasting destruction and shut out from the presence of the Lord and from the glory of his might."*

Salvation comes through faith alone, in Christ alone. When we embrace that truth, deep in our souls, we need never quiver in our boots when it comes to these so-called "scary verses" in Matthew 7.

That said, what these scary verses should do is drive us to our knees on behalf of those in our lives who have never put their trust in Jesus. They should compel us to clearly share the message of the gospel with everyone we know.

LIFE APPLICATION

Pray for a friend who needs Jesus. Then share the website Lifein6Words.com with someone who doesn't have a personal relationship with Jesus. Follow up and ask them what they think of the video.

20 GOD DOESN'T GRADE ON THE CURVE

What shall we conclude then? Do we have any advantage? Not at all! For we have already made the charge that Jews and Gentiles alike are all under the power of sin. As it is written:

> *"There is no one righteous, not even one;*
> *there is no one who understands;*
> *there is no one who seeks God.*
> *All have turned away,*
> *they have together become worthless;*
> *there is no one who does good,*
> *not even one."*
> *"Their throats are open graves;*
> *their tongues practice deceit."*
> *"The poison of vipers is on their lips."*
> *"Their mouths are full of cursing and bitterness."*
> *"Their feet are swift to shed blood;*
> *ruin and misery mark their ways,*
> *and the way of peace they do not know."*
> *"There is no fear of God before their eyes."*

Now we know that whatever the law says, it says to those who are under the law, so that every mouth may be silenced and the whole world held accountable to God. Therefore no one will be declared righteous in God's sight by the works of the law; rather, through the law we become conscious of our sin. Romans 3:9-20

In fourth grade, I cheated. I asked the kid next to me what 9 x 7 was. Mrs. Gallanger caught me, and sent me to my home room teacher, Mrs. Schrieber. I begged and pleaded with her not to tell my mom, and she reluctantly agreed.

Surprisingly, I still passed math that year. Why? Because as bad as I was, there were other kids who were worse than me. And this particular public school graded on the curve.

Grading on the curve measures a student not on what they know, but on how they compare to the rest of the class. Technically, you could get a 50%, and still get an A if most of the other kids scored lower than you.

The other more traditional approach to grading uses one set standard. Your grade is determined by whether you hit or miss a pre-established, uncompromising benchmark. This standards-based approach is used in most schools today.

> Bad as I was, there were other kids who were worse.

Did you know that God doesn't grade on the curve? Our natural human inclination is to look at others to see how we stack up in terms of being "good" or "bad." But God doesn't measure our performance based on how we compare with other people's performances. No, He has one uncompromising standard. His grading process is not "pass or fail," but " perfection or fail." He doesn't weigh our goodness against our badness, to see if we can squeak by with a 51%.

Revelation 21:27 makes it clear: *"Nothing impure will ever enter it* [heaven]." God's pure and holy nature demands that He set the standard for a pure and holy heaven at perfection. So if you don't get 100% right all the time, then you've flunked out.

In essence, this is what today's passage in Romans 3 is referring to. There's no way to pass God's class on our own. Why? Because we don't understand (verse 11), we don't seek God (verse 11), we don't do good (verse 12). We lie (verse 13). We're mean (verse 13). We're bitter and hurtful (verse 14). And we don't respect our teacher (verse 18).

If you don't get 100% right all the time, then you've flunked out.

But by His mercy, God's standards aren't there to crush us. They're there to point us in the right direction. Romans 3:20 puts it like this: *"Therefore no one will be declared righteous in God's sight by the works of the law; rather, through the law we become conscious of our sin."* For it is only when we become conscious of our sin, that we realize our desperate need for a Savior.

Truly embracing the gospel begins with knowing that we are destined to fail if we try to pass His class through our own efforts. It's impossible. Like a first grader at Harvard, who's been dropped into an Advanced Calculus class, we are more inclined toward squabbling over Lego® pieces, than mastering algorithms.

LIFE APPLICATION

Many people think you can earn your way into heaven by being "good enough." Initiate a conversation with someone in the next few days about what it takes to get to heaven. Here are some possible questions you might use as springboards to deeper conversation:

- What do you think happens after you die?
- Do you believe in heaven and hell?
- If there is a heaven, what do you think determines whether some someone goes to heaven or not?
- How does being "good enough" measure up against a holy God's standard of perfection?
- If you were to die tonight, do you know where you'd spend eternity?

PAYING

THE PRICE FOR SIN, AGAIN
JESUS DIED AND ROSE

But God demonstrates his
own love for us in this:
While we were still sinners,
Christ died for us.

- Romans 5:8

21 SNAKES, SKINS AND SALVATION

"And I will put enmity between you and the woman, and between your offspring and hers; he will crush your head, and you will strike his heel." Genesis 3:15

The Lord God made garments of skin for Adam and his wife and clothed them. Genesis 3:21

When I was 14 years old, I got my first job. I went with a group of my friends to buck hay in Texas for a summer.

It was the hardest job I've ever had.

We worked 12 hour days, six days a week in the blazing hot sun of the panhandle of Texas. To add insult to injury, we loaded, then unloaded, over 1,000 bales of hay per day by hand onto flatbed diesel trucks.

I'll never forget one field that was infested with snakes…rattlesnakes. Some of them got bound up in the hay bales. Others were underneath the bales that were being scooped up.

When my buddy, Duane, and I were instructed by our boss to get off the truck and roll the bales by hand into one long line, I was especially nervous. This city boy got baptized into country work pretty quickly, but seriously? This was more dangerous than running through my high crime rate neighborhood back home, waving a handful of hundred dollar bills in the air.

Then it happened. A rattlesnake came side-winding out from underneath a bale of hay. My buddy hit it with a hay hook, and then crushed its head. While the hay hook had stunned the snake, it was Duane's boot heel that actually killed the poisonous rattler.

Here in Genesis 3, we see something far more poisonous than a rattler on the loose. We see a spiritual battle shaping up that would impact all of human history.

God provided a foreshadowing of the outcome of the battle.

When God told the Snake (Satan), that He would put enmity (hatred) between him and the woman (Eve), and between his seed and her seed (Jesus), He was making it clear that a cosmic battle was going to ensue. But God also provided a foreshadowing of the outcome of that battle, indicating that Jesus would crush the serpent's head, although the snake would strike Jesus' heel.

This verse portends Jesus' death on the cross. When Jesus was crucified, it sounded the death knell for Satan... Although he is still alive and kicking, and can still wreak havoc on this earth, the guarantee of his ultimate destruction was secured at the cross.

That's why Satan used Peter to try to talk Jesus out of dying on the cross in Matthew 16, and why Jesus responded to Peter with such a harsh rebuke, saying *"Get behind me, Satan!"*

Colossians 2:15 describes what happened to the Devil when Jesus died on the cross: *"And having disarmed the powers and authorities, he made a public spectacle of them, triumphing over them by the cross."*

For those who put their trust in Christ, Jesus knocked the club of guilt and shame right out of the Devil's hands. In fact, He took out all of the Devil's best weapons when He declared, *"It is finished!"*

Jesus knocked the club of guilt and shame right out of the Devil's hands.

This foreshadowing of the cross in Genesis 3:15 has been labeled "the protevangel" by theologians, which means "first gospel." Isn't it amazing that immediately after the fall of Adam and Eve, we can see God setting His redemptive plan in motion?

And just six verses later we read, *"The Lord God made garments of skin for Adam and his wife and clothed them."* Do you see the implications of this? If God clothed them in animal skins, that means that He sacrificed the lives of animals to cover their shame and nakedness. God removed Adam and Eve's feeble, works-based, fig-leafed attempts to cover their guilt, and instead shed the blood of an innocent to cover their shame.

God *made* the first sacrifice. And God—in Jesus Christ—*was* the last (and lasting) sacrifice.

From the third chapter of Genesis, we see God' redemptive plan unfolding.

LIFE APPLICATION

Satan is still wreaking his havoc on earth. The world is full of people who are struggling with the pain and consequences of life in our broken world. Ask God to give you a heart that increasingly burns and breaks for the lost and broken.

Watch the short YouTube video "Why Does God Let Bad Things Happen?" found at somethingamazing.net/why. Prayerfully consider sharing it as a conversation starter with someone you know who is bitter, angry or disappointed with God because of the pain in their life.

22 PREVIEW OF A SAVIOR

...Jesus has become the guarantor of a better covenant.

Now there have been many of those priests, since death prevented them from continuing in office; but because Jesus lives forever, he has a permanent priesthood. Therefore he is able to save completely those who come to God through him, because he always lives to intercede for them.

Such a high priest truly meets our need—one who is holy, blameless, pure, set apart from sinners, exalted above the heavens. Unlike the other high priests, he does not need to offer sacrifices day after day, first for his own sins, and then for the sins of the people. He sacrificed for their sins once for all when he offered himself.
Hebrews 7: 22b-27

A coworker of mine once went to her daughter's Back to School night at a local public high school. While visiting the English Lit teacher's classroom, she was surprised to hear the teacher brazenly tell parents that if their teens weren't familiar with the Bible, they should go buy their students a children's book of Bible stories.

How could this public school teacher so boldly advocate that her students read stories from the Bible? Amid initial resistance from the more vocal non-Christian parents in the room, the teacher proceeded to make her case. It's virtually impossible, she explained, to understand the great classics of Western literature without some Bible literacy, for many are filled with Biblical allusions, symbolism and Christ-types. The multi-layered Biblical richness threaded throughout theses literary works can only be unlocked by a reader who knows enough to recognize them.

God threaded amazing multi-layered meaning throughout the Bible.

The author of the Bible—God Himself—also threaded some amazing multi-layered meaning across the 66 books of the Bible that were written by 40 different men, across a period of 1500 years. Today's Scripture passage offers an intriguing example of this.

In Old Testament times, the high priest served as an intermediary between God and the people for the forgiveness of their sins. Each year, on the Day of Atonement, only the high priest was allowed to enter the Holy of Holies, behind the veil of the temple, which separated sinful man from the presence of a holy God. There, in this sacred, holy, set-apart place, the priest sprinkled the blood of sacrificed animals on the mercy seat, God's throne. For *"without the shedding of blood there is no forgiveness"* (Hebrews 9:22).

With the coming of Christ and His atoning blood sacrifice on the cross, we see how Jesus became the *"once for all"* sacrifice for the sins of all people everywhere. At the very moment of Christ's death, the veil of the temple was ripped apart, dramatically symbolizing how Jesus opened the way for us to receive forgiveness for sins. Matthew 27:50-51a describes it like this, *"And when Jesus had cried out again in a loud voice, he gave up his spirit. At that moment the curtain of the temple was torn in two from top to bottom."*

The Old Testament priesthood would stop. But Jesus' priesthood will not. The Old Testament priesthood was temporal. Jesus' priesthood is eternal. The Old Testament priesthood could only temporarily cover over sin for a short time. Christ's priesthood ensured that sin is removed forever.

Jesus is the only intermediary we need to approach the mercy seat of God Almighty, and enter into a restored relationship with the holy and perfect One.

Jesus became the *"once for all"* sacrifice.

"…Jesus has become the guarantor of a better covenant."

Better than anything the Old Testament priests could offer.

LIFE APPLICATION

We have this hope as an anchor for the soul, firm and secure. It enters the inner sanctuary behind the curtain, where our forerunner, Jesus, has entered on our behalf. He has become a high priest forever… (Hebrews 6:19-20a).

As followers of Christ, you and I *"have this hope as an anchor for the soul, firm and secure."* Take a few moments, close your eyes and experience what it feels like deep in your soul to rest in this firm, safe, secure place. Thank Jesus for being your anchor.

Pray for someone you know who doesn't have Jesus as their anchor. Look for a way to open a spiritual dialogue with them. Perhaps you could start by asking them this simple question: "If there is a God, what do you think He wants from us?"

23 GOD HIMSELF WILL PROVIDE THE LAMB

Some time later God tested Abraham. He said to him, "Abraham!"

"Here I am," he replied.

Then God said, "Take your son, your only son, whom you love—Isaac—and go to the region of Moriah. Sacrifice him there as a burnt offering on a mountain I will show you."

Early the next morning Abraham got up and loaded his donkey. He took with him two of his servants and his son Isaac. When he had cut enough wood for the burnt offering, he set out for the place God had told him about. On the third day Abraham looked up and saw the place in the distance. He said to his servants, "Stay here with the donkey while I and the boy go over there. We will worship and then we will come back to you."

Abraham took the wood for the burnt offering and placed it on his son Isaac, and he himself carried the fire and the knife. As the two of them went on together, Isaac spoke up and said to his father Abraham, "Father?"

"Yes, my son?" Abraham replied.

"The fire and wood are here," Isaac said, "but where is the lamb for the burnt offering?"

Abraham answered, "God himself will provide the lamb for the burnt offering, my son." And the two of them went on together.

When they reached the place God had told him about, Abraham built an altar there and arranged the wood on it. He bound his son Isaac and laid him on the altar, on top of the wood. Then he reached out his hand and took the knife to slay his son. But the angel of the Lord called out to him from heaven, "Abraham! Abraham!"

"Here I am," he replied.

"Do not lay a hand on the boy," he said. "Do not do anything to him. Now I know that you fear God, because you have not withheld from me your son, your only son." Genesis 22:1-12

When I was a youngster, there were times my mom would call and call my name and get no response from me. Why? I was so engrossed in what I was doing that I had no ears to hear her calling. Sometimes, I think we're like this with God. We get so engrossed in our own myopic, daily lives, that we miss what God's trying to tell us.

So you have to love Abraham here. God says, "Abraham!" and Abraham responds immediately, not only with a 7 willing "Here I am," but with total obedience and trust—to the point of being willing to sacrifice his beloved son, if that was what God wanted him to do.

But this familiar story is more than just a recounting of one of the fathers of our faith being willing to sacrifice all for God. It's also a beautiful example of God threading multiple levels of meaning into this Old Testament story, for Isaac is a Christ-type.

Isaac is a Christ-type.

Here's how the *Baker Dictionary of Theology* describes this kind of Christ-type foreshadowing God has woven into Scripture: "A type is a shadow cast on the pages of Old Testament history by a truth whose full embodiment or antitype is found in the New Testament revelation" [5]

In what ways is Isaac a type of Christ? Let's take a look.

Both Isaac and Jesus were...

1. **Set apart for sacrifice**
   - **Isaac:** *"Sacrifice him there as a burnt offering on a mountain I will show you"* (Genesis 22:2).
   - **Jesus:** *"The next day John saw Jesus coming toward him and said, "Look, the Lamb of God, who takes away the sin of the world!" (John 1:29) and "God presented Christ as a sacrifice of atonement, through the shedding of his blood-to be received by faith"* (Romans 3:25a).

2. **Obedient to their fathers to the point of death**
   - **Isaac:** *"The fire and wood are here," Isaac said, "but where is the lamb for the burnt offering?"Abraham answered, "God himself will provide the lamb for the burnt offering, my son." And the two of them went on together.* (Genesis 22:7-8).
   - **Jesus:** *"And being found in appearance as a man, he humbled himself by becoming obedient to death—even death on a cross!"* (Philippians 2:8).

3. **Raised up by the power of God**
   - **Isaac:** *"Abraham reasoned that God could even raise the dead, and so in a manner of speaking he did receive Isaac back from death"* (Hebrews 11:19).
   - **Jesus:** *"...Christ was raised from the dead through the glory of the Father..."* (Romans 6:4).

So we can see that God's unfolding the Biblical narrative on multiple levels in Genesis 22! Abraham's willingness to obey God and sacrifice Isaac as a burnt offering is not just about Abraham's obedience to God, it's also a foreshadowing of the grand, sweeping, redemptive plan God's orchestrating across the pages of history.

LIFE APPLICATION

As the father of two children whom I dearly love, the story of Abraham trekking up the mountain to sacrifice his son, Isaac, sends a chill down my spine. But perhaps that was part of God's intent—to give us a picture we could begin to understand about the depth of the Father's great sacrifice for us, in sending His Son, Jesus, to pay the price for our sin.

Out of gratitude to Him, is there something He's calling you to put on the altar and sacrifice for Him? Take a few minutes and contemplate the following passage, then pray about what God may be calling you to sacrifice for Him today.

Therefore, I urge you, brothers and sisters, in view of God's mercy, to offer your bodies as a living sacrifice, holy and pleasing to God—this is your true and proper worship. Do not conform to the pattern of this world, but be transformed by the renewing of your mind. Then you will be able to test and approve what God's will is—his good, pleasing and perfect will (Romans 12:1-2).

24 HIS VERY NAME MEANS "SALVATION"

Then God ordered me, "Start all over: Love your wife again,
your wife who's in bed with her latest boyfriend, your
cheating wife.
Love her the way I, God, love the Israelite people,
even as they flirt and party with every god that takes their fancy."

I did it. I paid good money to get her back.
It cost me the price of a slave.
Then I told her, "From now on you're living with me.
No more whoring, no more sleeping around.
You're living with me and I'm living with you." Hosea 3:1-3 *(The Message)*

The sting of rejection when someone you love betrays you is an excruciatingly painful experience. My mom was married and divorced four times (at least that's how many I know about). As a youngster, I had a front row seat to the hurt and anger that erupt from the downward spiral of love-turned-to-rejection.

So the story of the Old Testament prophet, Hosea, and his steadfast, loyal love for his adulteress, prostitute wife, Gomer, amazes me—and all the more so because, once again, we see God weaving beautiful symbolism and foreshadowing into this story. For the story of Hosea's enduring love for his unfaithful wife symbolizes God's unwavering love for His sinful, rebellious people.

To give you some context, back in Hosea's day, the penalty for a woman caught in adultery was death by stoning. And Gomer had gone far beyond the sin of one adulterous affair, she'd had sex with a whole string of men. She was considered a prostitute. Even if she'd come crawling back to her husband, repentant, and begging for forgiveness, we could barely imagine that her husband might be willing to forgive her. That's what makes this story so arresting. It's while Gomer is still in full out rebellion that God tells

Hosea's enduring love for Gomer symbolizes God's love for us.

Hosea to go search for his wayward wife and bring her home. He finds her in the slave market, where he proceeds to buy her back, redeeming her from the life of a prostitute slave.

What a striking, symbolic picture this provides of God and us humans! Like Gomer, we have committed spiritual adultery and turned away from the God who created us to be with Him. We have abandoned our first love and willfully pushed God away. We've lusted after poor substitutes for the real, unfailing, eternal love of God—things like self, power, appearance, money and pleasure.

Yet, out of love for us, God willingly sent His Son, Jesus, into the "slave market" of the world, to buy us back and redeem us out of our bondage to sin and our penalty of death. We deserve judgment, but God is extending His love to us instead, through the atoning work Jesus did on the cross on our behalf. The salvation Jesus offers comes as a free gift from God. We can't earn it, all we can do is receive it, and then walk in the power of the cross and extend it to others in desperate need of it, too.

So, you see, Hosea is a Christ-type. In fact, Hosea's very name means "salvation." How cool is that?

LIFE APPLICATION

Love isn't always easy. In fact, sometimes it's painfully hard to love those who push you to your limit. Yet God calls us to love even our very enemies—which is absolutely impossible in our own strength. That's why we must plug into the power of the Holy Spirit. Only He can work in us to produce the kind of love that *"never fails"* and *"keeps no record of wrongs"* (1 Corinthians 13).

Hosea demonstrated a depth of love for the "unlovable" that only comes from God. How about you? Is there someone "unlovable" in your life that you know God wants you to love with the love of Christ?

Spend some time right now praying for that person. Then look for ways in the coming days to consciously demonstrate the love of Christ to them—with no expectation that they will appreciate your sacrificial efforts or love you in return.

25 FASTER THAN A SPEEDING BULLET...

In your relationships with one another, have the same mindset as Christ Jesus: Who, being in very nature God, did not consider equality with God something to be used to his own advantage; rather, he made himself nothing by taking the very nature of a servant, being made in human likeness. And being found in appearance as a man, he humbled himself by becoming obedient to death—even death on a cross!
Philippians 2:5-8

In the beginning was the Word, and the Word was with God, and the Word was God.
John 1:1

The Word became flesh and made his dwelling among us. John 1:14a

As a child, I used to love to watch episodes of *Superman*. I couldn't wait to hear the words "Faster than a speeding bullet! More powerful than a locomotive! Able to leap tall buildings in a single bound! Look! Up in the sky! It's a bird! It's a plane! It's Superman!" These words cued his entrance to save the day.

Superman was from another world (Krypton), but he disguised his true identity by dressing like the nerdy reporter Clark Kent. Looking like an everyday Joe allowed him to masquerade as a human. But when calamity struck and aliens invaded or monsters attacked, he would find himself a phone booth and transform into Superman.

Sometimes, we wrongly view Jesus as Superman. We view Him as God, and rightfully so. But sometimes, it's almost as though we think that Jesus just "dressed up" as a human. We view him as a kind of Jewish Clark Kent. We know where he's really from... and it ain't Bethlehem. He's from Planet Paradise.

But here's the problem, Jesus is not Superman! Jesus is way more complex and mysterious. He is from heaven AND earth. He is human AND divine. He is 100% man AND 100% God.

Jesus is not Superman!

I'm convinced that most of us tend to way underestimate the humanity of Jesus. But if we look at the gospels closely, we see that Jesus got hungry (Mark 11:12), thirsty (John 19:28) and tired (John 4:6). He was every bit as human as you and I are. Jesus had to wait in line, use the restroom, sleep at night and do chores when he was a kid.

All it takes to see how fully human Jesus was, is a quick look at His three hour wrestling match with the Father in prayer in the Garden of Gethsemane. Here's how Luke 22:39-44 describes it: *"Jesus went out as usual to the Mount of Olives, and his disciples followed him. On reaching the place, he said to them, 'Pray that you will not fall into temptation.' He withdrew about a stone's throw beyond them, knelt down and prayed, 'Father, if you are willing, take this cup from me; yet not my will, but yours be done.' An angel from heaven appeared to him and strengthened him. And being in anguish, he prayed more earnestly, and his sweat was like drops of blood falling to the ground."*

Jesus' intense three hour struggle in that garden serves as a microcosm for the three plus years of ministry that he battled through on His knees in prayer. He found guidance from the Scriptures (like we do), depended on the Spirit (like we should) and found His strength in God (like we get to!).

Did Jesus ever sin? No! Hebrews 4:15 makes this clear, *"For we do not have a high priest who is unable to empathize with our weaknesses, but we have one who has been tempted in every way, just as we are—yet he did not sin."*

Jesus was God in the flesh. Jesus was not Superman, but the God-man. As a full—and sinless—human, He could die for other humans. As God, His payment for sin was infinite.

But even beyond salvation, there are some amazing implications that flow out of Jesus being fully God and fully human. Because He is the God-man, we can pray with the absolute boldness Hebrews 4:16 describes, *"Let us then approach God's throne of grace with confidence, so that we may receive mercy and find grace to help us in our time of need."*

Because Jesus suffered, and was tempted, He can empathize with us when we ask Him for help. Scripture tells us that He was tempted in every way we are. As a matter of fact, I'm thinking that if you and I are attacked by Satan at a Level 2, then Jesus was probably attacked at a Level 10. When He was tested in the wilderness in Matthew 4:1-11, He suffered the worst that Satan could throw at Him, yet was without sin.

He can empathize with us when we ask Him for help.

As a result, Jesus absolutely relates with us in our weaknesses, temptations and trials. And He will be there to intercede with the Father on our behalf, as one who relates to our struggles.

We have an ally. We have an intercessor. We have a Savior.

We don't need no Superman.

LIFE APPLICATION

Do you sometimes feel like God doesn't understand your character weaknesses and sin struggles? Re-read Hebrews 4:15-16, *"For we do not have a high priest who is unable to empathize with our weaknesses, but we have one who has been tempted in every way, just as we are—yet he did not sin. Let us then approach God's throne of grace with confidence, so that we may receive mercy and find grace to help us in our time of need."*

Jesus empathizes with our weaknesses. He's not a judging, blaming, finger-pointing, cosmic policeman. He knows you, understands your struggles, and loves you—warts and all. Of course, God also loves you too much to leave you where you are in the muck and mud of your sin. That's why God sent the Holy Spirit. So thank Him for His forgiveness, then ask the Spirit to show you one particular area of temptation in your life that it's time to face head on. Ask Him to provide the wisdom, power, strength and strategies you'll need to stand firm when temptation comes your way.

26 PAID IN FULL

When you were dead in your sins and in the uncircumcision of your flesh, God made you alive with Christ. He forgave us all our sins, having canceled the charge of our legal indebtedness, which stood against us and condemned us; he has taken it away, nailing it to the cross. Colossians 2:13-14

Maybe you know that sinking feeling. You're driving down the road with a heavy foot, trying to get somewhere on time. Suddenly you go over the hill, and as you descend, you see the police car positioned just right. The cop has his radar gun pointed right at you, and you know you're gonna get a ticket.

Unfortunately, that's happened to me more times than I'd like to remember. Yes, I'm a preacher who likes to drive with intentionality and "godspeed."

But one day, after getting a speeding ticket, something really weird happened. I got a copy of my ticket sent back to me in the mail with a cancellation note on it…and a smiley face.

Somebody at ticket-giving headquarters paid the bill and cancelled the ticket. To this day, I have no idea who. All I know is that it reminds me of Colossians 2:13-14.

God has *"cancelled the charge"* of our sin debt, only we know full well who paid our penalty—Jesus! He wrote a check with His life when He died on the cross and paid for all our misdeeds and mess-ups—past, present and future.

In Jesus' final moments on the cross, He made a bold declaration when He uttered a single word: *"Tetelastai"* (John 19:30). Most Bibles translate this single word into the phrase, *"It is finished."* But in the original language, it has deeper, richer meaning, for it can also be translated as *"Paid in full."*

In New Testament times, the word *tetelestai* was written on business documents to indicate that a bill had been "paid in full." And that's exactly what Jesus did on the cross for us—He set us free from the penalty we were under because of our sin. Ephesians 1:7-8 puts it like this: *Because of the sacrifice of the Messiah, his blood poured out on the altar of the Cross, we're a free people—free of penalties and punishments chalked up by all our misdeeds. And not just barely free, either. Abundantly free! (The Message).*

We're declared not just barely free, but totally free! *"Abundantly free!"*

> # We're declared not just barely free, but totally free!

Do you feel totally free from the burden of guilt and shame for your sins? Many Christians continue to struggle with a nagging voice inside their head, telling them that they'll never be good enough for God to really love them and totally forgive them.

Yet God tells you differently. God tells you your penalty has been *"paid in full"*!

LIFE APPLICATION

Are you living like you are *"abundantly free"*? Does God's grace shine through your every attitude and action? As forgiven followers of Jesus, we should be the most joy-filled people on the planet! As you read each of the following Bible verses, pause and talk to God about each.

1 John 1:9 *If we confess our sins, He is faithful and just and will forgive us our sins and purify us from all unrighteousness.*

Romans 8:1 *Therefore, there is now no condemnation for those who are in Christ Jesus.*

Psalm 103:12 *As far as the east is from the west, so far has he removed our transgressions from us.*

Think about how you'd feel if you were under a crushing debt burden—say you owed someone a million dollars. Then imagine how you'd react if you found out that your massive debt had been totally cancelled and forgiven. You'd be pretty excited, right?

Jesus' forgiveness is worth infinitely more than $1,000,000!

So go live your life today in light of the awesome reality that your sin debt has been *"paid in full"*! Be joyful, be generous, be exuberant as you walk through your day. Let your unbounded joy flow out of the depth of your soul!

27 REASONS TO BELIEVE

For what I received I passed on to you as of first importance: that Christ died for our sins according to the Scriptures, that he was buried, that he was raised on the third day according to the Scriptures, and that he appeared to Cephas [Peter], *and then to the Twelve. After that, he appeared to more than five hundred of the brothers and sisters at the same time, most of whom are still living, though some have fallen asleep.* 1 Corinthians 15:3-6

"How can you be so sure that the God of the Bible is the one, true God?" As I talk to people about Jesus, I hear this question a lot.

So how do you know? How can you know? Let me tell you how I know.

As a young child, I often found myself staring up into the sky looking at the stars. I remember thinking that all this had to come from Someone way bigger than me. That Someone had to be big, strong, smart and totally in control. That Someone had to be God. Little did I know that I was engaging in what some call "The Teleological Argument." It simply goes like this: design requires a designer.

When I trusted in Jesus as my Savior as a youngster, through His Spirit, He came to live inside my soul. He gave me hope, purpose and forgiveness. While the changes I saw Him make in my life may not have been enough to prove His existence to others, they were more than enough to prove to me that God was real.

But then I started studying His Word and I began to sense that it was truth. And it claimed again and again to be the truth, the God inspired truth (Proverbs 30:5; John 17:17; 2 Timothy 3:16).

As I grew older and began to share my faith in my early teens, I would point my friends to the sky, tell them about the difference Jesus made in my life, and then take them to the Scriptures. Some of them believed. But some of them did not. They asked me questions like:

How can you be so sure that the God of the Bible is the one, true God?

- "How do you know your experiences are any more valid than someone from a different religion?"
- "So what if the Bible claims to be the truth, so does *The Book of Mormon* and *The Koran*. What makes the Bible true?"
- "How do you know that your God is the right God?"

As I've wrestled with these kinds of questions over the years, I've found three reasons to believe.

1. Creation

God created an amazing earth, a breathtaking sky and a marvelous, massive universe to get everyone's attention. That's His bullhorn that shouts, "I am here and I am not silent! This is not an accident! All of this was made by design!" You don't look at a beautiful painting and think "Wow, what an accident!" You think, "Wow, what an artist!" The same is true of the ultimate masterpiece, the universe itself. There had to be a big brain behind the intricate design of it all. There had to be a big power behind it all to make the concept a reality. From the amazing human body, to the vastness of the universe, to the surprisingly complex world of the micro universe (protons, neutrons, quarks, etc.), there has to be a Designer.

2. The Bible

The Bible was written over the course of 1,500 years by the pen of 40 different authors from all sorts of cultural backgrounds, yet it's entirely without contradiction or errors.

The only way that could happen is that it was completely inspired by God Himself. Anyone could claim to have written a holy book (Joseph Smith, Mohammed, etc.), but this book was not the brain child of one person with a vivid imagination.

The Bible is not only internally consistent, it is packed with prophecies that support its claim of being divinely inspired. Did you know that the Old Testament contains over three hundred prophecies about Jesus that were literally and fully fulfilled in him? These aren't wussy prophecies that are relatively unclear and written in a way that could be taken in several different ways. These are specific prophecies like:

- The place where Jesus would be born (Micah 5:2)
- That He would be born of a virgin (Isaiah 7:14)
- How Jesus would die (Psalm 22)
- That He would rise again (Psalm 16:8-11)

And on and on and on the list goes.

3. Jesus' resurrection
Jesus appeared to over 500 people after He rose from the dead. Many of them were willing to die for their faith. As someone has said, many will die for what they think to be the truth, but nobody will die for what they know to be a lie. The early martyrs who had seen Jesus after His resurrection were willing to die for what they knew to be the truth…He is alive!

So why do I believe in the God of the Bible?

I see His handiwork in the sky. I sense His presence in my soul. I've seen the difference in my life. I read His book that is perfect and amazing and a miracle in and of itself. I read the fulfilled prophecies that could never be predicted without God providing the insight into the future. I embrace the resurrected Jesus, the same Jesus that the early

Christians were willing to die for because they were eyewitnesses of His presence. And that resurrected Jesus has transformed my life.

My reasons for believing are part relational, part rational and part experiential. The relational and experiential were enough for me to believe in Jesus on June 23rd, 1974. But the rational reasons to believe gave me more confidence over the years that my faith was more than just a personal belief. It was the truth. God gave proof of this faith as the true faith by raising Jesus from the dead.

My reasons for believing are relational, rational and experiential.

Whether your faith in God is primarily relational, experiential, rational, or a combination of all three, you have full-bodied, multi-dimensional reasons to stake your life on the God of the Bible. These reasons encompass your heart, soul and mind. They range from the beauty in the sky, to fulfilled prophecies, to personal transformation, to the warm fuzzies in your heart when you think about Him. Isn't it just like God to give us every reason to believe in Him with every level of our humanity?

LIFE APPLICATION

Jesus has called every single one of His followers to be His ambassadors. It's our mission in life to share our reasons to believe with everyone around us.

To help you prepare for this mission, check out the training sections of the Dare 2 Share mobile app. It's packed with video training and tools that will help you learn how to share your faith in your own unique way. You can find it at dare2share.org/mobileapp.

EVERYONE

WHO TRUSTS IN HIM LIFE
ALONE HAS ETERNAL

For God so loved the world that
he gave his one and only Son,
that whoever believes in him shall
not perish but have eternal life.

- John 3:16

28 THE SHORTEST SERMON EVER PREACHED

He went to Nazareth, where he had been brought up, and on the Sabbath day he went into the synagogue, as was his custom. He stood up to read, and the scroll of the prophet Isaiah was handed to him. Unrolling it, he found the place where it is written:

> *"The Spirit of the Lord is on me,*
> *because he has anointed me*
> *to proclaim good news to the poor.*
> *He has sent me to proclaim freedom for the prisoners*
> *and recovery of sight for the blind,*
> *to set the oppressed free,*
> *to proclaim the year of the Lord's favor."*

Then he rolled up the scroll, gave it back to the attendant and sat down. The eyes of everyone in the synagogue were fastened on him. He began by saying to them, "Today this scripture is fulfilled in your hearing." Luke 4:16-21

Prisons come in all sorts of shapes and sizes. They can be as small as our own hearts and as large as the worldwide web that sucks people into the prison of porn addiction. The Evil One specializes in taking everyday things and twisting them into prisons of despair and death.

One such instance that's seared into my memory is the day the Columbine High School shootings unfolded, turning a local high school in my city into a prison, of sorts. Living just minutes away from the scene of the tragedy, I watched and prayed as the unfolding horror filled the TV screen. Students and teachers were trapped in the school while a pair of young gunmen brought death and destruction to this quiet, middle class suburban neighborhood. Hundreds of parents waited, desperate to hear whether their teenagers were among those who'd found their way out of the school to freedom.

In today's Scripture passage, Jesus quotes an Old Testament messianic passage written by the prophet Isaiah, which speaks of the prison of spiritual captivity. For centuries, the Jewish people had heard this passage read in their synagogues. They believed that

Prisons come in all sorts of shapes and sizes.

it prophesied a long-promised Messiah who would come as a ruling, triumphant savior for their people. The Jews were looking for a political figure who would arrive on the scene to *"proclaim freedom for the prisoners"* and *"set the oppressed free."*

Imagine the shock when Jesus boldly, yet simply stated, *"Today this scripture is fulfilled in your hearing."* Jesus is declaring that He is the One. He is the long-promised Messiah— the only one who can bring ultimate deliverance—spiritual deliverance from the prison of sin we humans find ourselves enslaved in.

Jesus is the One who brings real liberty. Only by putting our faith and trust in Him alone will the spiritual chains of sin and death that bind us fall off. Jesus said, *"I am the way and the truth and the life. No one comes to the Father except through me"* (John 14:6). He is the only way out of our spiritual prison, throwing the door wide open into the place of freedom we have in Christ. He is our hope for heaven and eternal life with God.

Now that really is good news worth proclaiming!

The Columbine High School massacre triggered a pivotal turning point in my career. I couldn't help but think how things might have been different if only those two troubled

Jesus is the One who brings real liberty.

teenage gunmen had heard the good news of the gospel from another teen they knew and trusted.

So following the shooting, I resigned my position as a church pastor to pursue the ministry of Dare 2 Share (D2S) full-time, a ministry that is committed to mobilizing teens to evangelize their world. Since then, through the ministry of D2S, hundreds of thousand of teenagers across the country have been motivated and equipped to relationally reach out to those who don't know Jesus with the gospel message of hope.

LIFE APPLICATION

While God may not be calling you to quit your job so you can do evangelism full-time, He may be nudging you to gently, lovingly share the gospel with someone specific who is living in the spiritual prison of discouragement or hopelessness. Pray and ask God how you can be an encouragement to someone like that today. Then look for an opportunity to share about Jesus' freedom for the prisoners.

29 YOU MUST BE WICKED

However, to the man who does not work but trusts God who justifies the wicked, his faith is credited as righteousness. Romans 4:5 (NIV, 1984)

My Uncle Jack was wicked, by his own admission. He spent hard time in prison for choking two cops unconscious when they were trying to arrest him on domestic abuse charges. He was a fighter. He was a drinker. He was a partier. In his younger years, he was routinely in trouble with rival gangs and angry police officers.

On a dare, a preacher from the suburbs nicknamed "Yankee" (although he spoke with a southern accent...long story), knocked on Uncle Jack's door one day. Yankee explained that one of his Christian friends had dared him to come tell Jack about Jesus.

Surprisingly, Jack let this preacher into his house. Shirtless and tattooed, with a beer can in each hand—one for beer and the other for spitting chewing tobacco—Jack invited Yankee to sit down with him at the kitchen table.

Jack was expecting a religious talk, but he got something else, instead. He heard that Jesus died for the wicked...just like him. You see, my Uncle Jack had always thought heaven was for the good people, for the religious folks who dressed up on Sundays and went to church with the rest of the do-gooders. Jack figured he didn't make the cut, and would most assuredly go to hell. He figured he might as well party it up while he could.

But Yankee shared a different message—that Jesus came to save sinners. All Jack had to do was believe and receive. Believe that Jesus died for him, and receive the free gift of eternal life.

When Yankee asked him if this message made sense, he enthusiastically screamed, "Hell, YES!!!" This became Jack's sinner's prayer, and from that very moment, he began a journey of transformation. I witnessed Uncle Jack's transformation when I was just a little kid in North Denver. And I immediately knew that if Jesus could save my Uncle Jack, He could save anybody…even me.

If Jesus could save my Uncle Jack, He could save anybody.

In Mark 2:17, Jesus tells us, *"It is not the healthy who need a doctor, but the sick. I have not come to call the righteous, but sinners."*

Take a closer look at the gospels, and you'll see that Jesus hung out with hookers, tax collectors and sinners, the very "scum" of society. Why? Because that's who He came to seek and to save.

Take a closer look at today's verse, Romans 4:5, and you'll see three simple requirements for salvation:

1. You must not work.
"…to the man who does not work…."

Those who think they can earn their way into God's good graces don't understand God's grace. Grace, by definition, is free and unearned. Doing something to earn it is like trying to pay back somebody for a gift given on Christmas—which is like a slap in the face to the giver.

2. You must trust God.
"…to the man who does not work but trust God…."

Salvation is not a matter of trying, but of trusting. It's not a matter of what we do, but what Jesus has done. We come to God, knowing that we have nothing to bring to the table. And with simple childlike faith, we trust in Him to save us, based on the death, burial and resurrection of Jesus. Then He saves us.

Years ago, the ministry I lead pulled off a one-of-a-kind project. Dare 2 Share did a reality series called *Gospel Journey Maui*. Via an ad on Craig's List, we pulled together a Mormon, Muslim, Buddhist, Jewish dude, Seventh Day Adventist, a girl who thought God was a black woman who baked cookies (based on the oracle character in *The Matrix*) and a surfing evangelical believer named Zane Black.

For eight days in Maui, we surfed, zip lined down volcanoes, explored the scenery and had spiritual discussions. Jasser, the young Muslim man, was especially committed to his belief system. He was sure that praying five times a day toward Mecca, along with keeping the other pillars of Islam, would help him earn his eternal life.

Salvation is not a matter of trying, but of trusting.

After zip lining a huge course on the side of Haleakula, the resident volcano, I asked Jasser what he had to do to make it to the other side of the course. He said all he had to do was trust the zip line. Then I asked him, "What if you tried to make it across the zip line by using your bare hands to carry yourself across?" He said that he would never make it, because it was way too far for anyone to carry themselves across by hand. I agreed. Then I shared with him that salvation was the same way. If we try to do it by our own strength, we are sure to fail, because the standard is way too far for any human to make—perfection. But if we take the zip line approach, and simply trust in Jesus, He will carry us across.

3. You must be wicked.
"…to the man who does not work but trusts God who justifies the wicked, his faith is credited as righteousness."

I love the use of the word "wicked" in this passage. We're not talking just about those who are mistaken, or struggling with poor choices, or just a little bad. We're talking about full-on, rage-against-God sinners. God only justifies the wicked who actually realize they are wicked. Those who think they are righteous are wicked too. They just refuse to acknowledge it, and therefore have no need for a Savior.

But when we see ourselves as wicked, quit trying to save ourselves through our own efforts and simply put our faith in Jesus, we are justified—declared righteous.

Does that sound like good news?

Hell, yes!

LIFE APPLICATION

Ask yourself the following questions:

1. Are you "working" to earn God's forgiveness for your sins, misdeeds and mess-ups?
2. Are you trusting God with simple, childlike faith?
3. Do you freely acknowledge your "wickedness" before God and actively fall solely upon His mercy and grace?

30 CHILDLIKE FAITH

At that time the disciples came to Jesus and asked, "Who, then, is the greatest in the kingdom of heaven?"

He called a little child to him, and placed the child among them. And he said: "Truly I tell you, unless you change and become like little children, you will never enter the kingdom of heaven. Therefore, whoever takes the lowly position of this child is the greatest in the kingdom of heaven. Matthew 18:1-4

When my daughter, Kailey, was very young, she loved to jump into my outstretched arms with wild abandon. She'd jump from anywhere and everywhere. Whether she was hurling herself from the stairs above me, or from climbing equipment on a playground, there was never the slightest hesitation on her part. She was fearless. Why? Because she had absolutely no doubt that I would catch her.

She had a simple, childlike faith in her daddy's willingness and ability to catch her.

That's the kind of total, trusting confidence Jesus is talking about here in Matthew 18 when it comes to the kingdom of heaven.

It all started when the disciples were wondering what it takes to be to be *"the greatest in the kingdom."* In Luke 9:46, the wording is a little more colorful. It says, " *An argument started among the disciples as to which of them would be the greatest."*

So they are not asking this question because they want to contribute the most they possibly can to the advancement of the kingdom. They're asking because they want to know how best to jockey for position, strive for maximum advantage and climb the ladder of advancement. They're wondering what they need to do to land a place of prominence and come out as top dog.

But here's Jesus, turning their egotistical posturing totally on its head, by responding with a beautiful, yet simple, object lesson. As He draws a little child into the circle of conversation, He says, *"Unless you change and become like little children, you will never enter the kingdom of heaven. Therefore, whoever takes the lowly position of this child is the greatest in the kingdom of heaven."*

God wants you to run to Him as your heavenly Daddy.

What is Jesus driving at here? That we must come to God with the simple, humble, trusting dependence of a child. Access to the kingdom of heaven comes only when we rely entirely on our heavenly Father's caring provision for us. We must put our faith and trust in Jesus alone for our salvation. No amount of striving and jockeying on our part will help us "earn" our way into the kingdom of heaven. It is simply and only by FAITH, and faith alone, that we receive the free gift of eternal life.

We must "change our minds" (that's what the word "repent" means, by the way) about who we are before God, and recognize our need for a Savior to rescue us from our sin. Then we must totally and completely trust our heavenly daddy to catch us as we fall into His outstretched arms. He is willing, eager and able to save us.

LIFE APPLICATION

Over and over again in Scripture—hundreds of times, actually—both in the Old Testament and in the New, those of us who trust in God are referred to as children of God. Are you experiencing the beauty and simplicity of that kind of father-child relationship with God? Go through the following list that describes those who trust in the Triune God of the Bible as children of God. One by one, reflect on the implications of each label for your own life:

- Children of promise
- Children of the day
- Children of light
- Dear children
- Little children
- Beloved children

31 THE PRODIGAL

Jesus continued: "There was a man who had two sons. The younger one said to his father, 'Father, give me my share of the estate.' So he divided his property between them.

"Not long after that, the younger son got together all he had, set off for a distant country and there squandered his wealth in wild living. After he had spent everything, there was a severe famine in that whole country, and he began to be in need. So he went and hired himself out to a citizen of that country, who sent him to his fields to feed pigs. He longed to fill his stomach with the pods that the pigs were eating, but no one gave him anything.

"When he came to his senses, he said, 'How many of my father's hired servants have food to spare, and here I am starving to death! I will set out and go back to my father and say to him: Father, I have sinned against heaven and against you. I am no longer worthy to be called your son; make me like one of your hired servants.' So he got up and went to his father.

"But while he was still a long way off, his father saw him and was filled with compassion for him; he ran to his son, threw his arms around him and kissed him.

"The son said to him, 'Father, I have sinned against heaven and against you. I am no longer worthy to be called your son.'

"But the father said to his servants, 'Quick! Bring the best robe and put it on him. Put a ring on his finger and sandals on his feet. Bring the fattened calf and kill it. Let's have a feast and celebrate. For this son of mine was dead and is alive again; he was lost and is found.' So they began to celebrate.

"Meanwhile, the older son was in the field. When he came near the house, he heard music and dancing. So he called one of the servants and asked him what was going on. 'Your brother has come,' he replied, 'and your father has killed the fattened calf because he has him back safe and sound.'

"The older brother became angry and refused to go in. So his father went out and pleaded with him. But he answered his father, 'Look! All these years I've been slaving for you and never disobeyed your orders. Yet you never gave me even a young goat so I could celebrate with my friends. But when this son of yours who has squandered your property with prostitutes comes home, you kill the fattened calf for him!'

"'My son,' the father said, 'you are always with me, and everything I have is yours. But we had to celebrate and be glad, because this brother of yours was dead and is alive again; he was lost and is found.'" Luke 15:11-32

Jesus' parable of the patient, loving Father and the two sons who thought they had life figured out on their own terms shows us a lot about God and a lot about ourselves.

Like the two brothers, we humans tend to approach life in one of these two ways:

It's actually the older brother who may be the most "lost."

- We pursue the self-absorbed, indulgent life which is all about me—consequences be damned; or
- We pursue the moral life, often on our own terms, through our own strength, for our own purposes, trying to "earn" our way into God's good graces. Which is also, at its root, all about me being good enough—except that we're sinning without looking like it on the outside.

In this story, it's the younger brother who is the first to figure out that he's "lost." That's why he heads for home. Sadly, it's actually the older brother who may be the most "lost"—for his pride and self-righteousness keep him from recognizing his need.

He's blind to the reality that instead of compassion, he carries only resentment. Instead of being grace-giving, he is busy judging and comparing. He can't see that he's been doing the right things for the wrong reasons—out of duty to his father, instead of out of love for Him.

You see, God wants a totally different kind of life for us than either of these two brothers represent. He wants RELATIONSHIP! Not a cordial, friendly, transactional relationship with us, but an intimate, authentic, love relationship that draws us together with Him at the deepest level of our very souls.

All is forgiven, if only we will run into His outstretched arms.

Whether we've lived the life of the younger brother, or the older one, our loving, forgiving Heavenly Father stands with arms outstretched, inviting us into that kind of radical, life-changing relationship. All is forgiven, if only we will run into His outstretched arms and join His party!

For it's only when we begin to understand that both our blatant sins **and** our moral strivings to make God like us are obstacles to a true, deep, trust-filled, loving, soul-quenching relationship with God. When we truly get that, then we're truly starting to grasp how incredibly radical the message of the gospel is.

God wants us to love and serve Him not out of duty, but out of deep, genuine, overflowing gratitude for who He is to us. He wants our love, not only because of what He's done for us, but for who He is. That's what moves us from God as "boss," to God as "Father."

LIFE APPLICATION

Spend some time reflecting on the following questions:

- What makes this parable of Jesus so totally scandalous?
- Do you view God as "boss" or as "Father"?
- Are you consistently running toward God's outstretched, welcoming embrace?

32 "STAND UPON THE CHAIR!"

And if by grace, then it cannot be based on works; if it were, grace would no longer be grace. Romans 11:6

Jesus answered, "I am the way and the truth and the life. No one comes to the Father except through me." John 14:6

"Salvation is found in no one else, for there is no other name under heaven given to mankind by which we must be saved." Acts 4:12

Twenty four years ago, I was in India as a newly married preacher/evangelist. I was there at the invitation of a seasoned evangelist who needed a preaching partner. It was my first time out of the country, and I had no missions training whatsoever. So, to put it bluntly, I was a little bit like a bull in a China closet, or a steer in an Indian restaurant, or something like that.

During my 18 days on the ground there, I preached 56 times. It was trial and error. One time, I put offering money in the wrong bowl. Another time, a Hindu leader stormed the stage and tried to wrangle the microphone from my hand as I preached the gospel—unsuccessfully, I might add. But through prayer and persistence, I finally figured out an approach that seemed to work, especially when talking to Hindu teenagers.

It was kind of a strange situation. The Catholic schools we were invited to were not legally allowed to preach the gospel to their mostly Hindu students. But at the time, guest preachers *could* share the gospel. So the priests running these schools were thrilled when their crazy Protestant cousin (yours truly), would lay out the Christian gospel for their students.

Early on, I learned that, many times, Hindu students respond to the gospel message by just adding Jesus to their shelves full of gods, because Hinduism is a polytheistic religion. So I racked my brain to think of a way to help these teenagers realize that Jesus was the only way of salvation. Finally, an idea struck pay dirt.

Before I'd start preaching, I'd place a chair on the stage somewhere. After I shared the gospel, I'd say something like, "Now children, (even teenagers were called children in this culture), what is this?"

"It is a chair!" they'd yell.

"When Jesus says that we must believe in Him to be saved, He means that we must trust in Him and Him alone, and in nothing and nobody else but Him to forgive us for our sins."

You can't trust in Jesus *plus* any other God.

Then I'd take one foot, put it on the seat part of the chair and ask, "Am I trusting fully in this chair?"

For some reason, the audience invariably roared with laughter and "no's" would echo across the boisterous, school-uniformed audience.

"What do I need to do to truly show that I'm trusting in it?" I'd ask.

And the audience would yell in near unison, "Stand upon the chair!!!"

I'd stand with both feet on the chair and the crowd went wild—again, I don't quite know why, but they thought it was great.

"Now, am I trusting in the chair!!!" I'd ask.

"YES!!!" they'd yell together.

Then I'd make my point, "In the same way, you can't trust in Jesus **plus** any other god. When you put your faith in Him, you are putting your faith in Jesus alone for your salvation. Otherwise, you just have one foot on the chair. Otherwise, you are not really trusting in Him." Then I gave the rest of the gospel, and the invitation, while standing on top of the chair.

Jesus offers an exclusive message, in a very inclusive way.

Many young people indicated faith in Jesus, during that three week trip. Many were rescued from the bondage of Hinduism, and given new hope through Christ.

But today in Western culture, there is another, milder form of Eastern mysticism creeping in. Although not technically Hinduism, it is the belief system that says whatever god you worship is fine, and if you don't worship any god, that's fine too. As long as you're a nice person, don't judge others and are sincere in your beliefs, you'll probably make it to heaven or Nirvana or whatever.

The problem is that Jesus offers an exclusive message, in a very inclusive way.

It's exclusive in the sense that Jesus said, *"No one comes to the Father except through me"* (John 14:6). But He offers eternal life to anyone and everyone *"who believes in him"* (John 3:16).

As we share the good news of the gospel in this culture, we must encourage friends, neighbors, classmates and coworkers to "stand upon the chair" by putting both feet on the finished work of Christ on the cross.

All other ground is sinking sand.

LIFE APPLICATION

"Jesus answered, 'I am the way and the truth and the life. No one comes to the Father except through me.'" Does the exclusivist nature of Jesus' words here in John 14:6 make you uncomfortable? If so, have a conversation with God about it.

We all know people who need to hear that Jesus is the way, they truth and the life. Pray and ask God for wisdom and courage. Then step out and get the conversation started.

For help doing this, I encourage you to check out the spiritual conversation starting YouTube video, "Have You Ever Wondered About God?" You can find the video here: somethingamazing.net/God. Email it, text it, post it or whatever work best for you. Follow up with a "Let's talk, I want to know what you think…"

33 THE GREAT EXCHANGE

God made him who had no sin to be sin for us, so that in him we might become the righteousness of God. 2 Corinthians 5:21

You've probably seen the signs. They're often posted around town on telephone poles. "Cash for junk." Junk cars, that is.

What a great exchange, when you can give someone something you wanted to get rid of anyway, and swap it for something of value.

Trash for treasure. Sin for righteousness. Your sinful garbage exchanged for the riches of a restored relationship with a righteous, holy and perfect God. 2 Corinthians 5:21 communicates the very heart of the gospel message.

The Great Exchange set you free. He willingly bore your sin, suffered and died, so that you might live in close, intimate relationship with Him now and forever.

The Message paraphrase of Ephesians 2:4-9 describes the Great Exchange like this: *"...Immense in mercy and with an incredible love, he embraced us. He took our sin-dead lives and made us alive in Christ. He did all this on his own, with no help from us! Then he picked us up and set us down in highest heaven in company with Jesus, our Messiah. Now God has us where he wants us, with all the time in this world and the next to shower grace and kindness upon us in Christ Jesus. Saving is all his idea, and all his work. All we do is trust him enough to let him do it. It's God's gift from start to finish! We don't play the major role. If we did, we'd probably go around bragging that we'd done the whole thing! No, we neither make nor save ourselves. God does both the making and saving."*

Why did God do this for you when you don't deserve it? Because of His incredible love for you! Jesus didn't *have* to die on the cross. He willingly **chose** to die on the cross. He wasn't a helpless victim. He was a God-man on a rescue mission. In John 10:18, Jesus says, *"No one takes it* [my life] *from me, but I lay it down of my own accord. I have authority to lay it down and authority to take it up again..."* Jesus is making it clear that He would rather die a horrible, painful death on the cross, than live without you.

Trash for treasure. Sin for righteousness.

He had no guarantee that you would accept His love, His sacrifice and His gift of eternal life when He set about His rescue plan for the Great Exchange. Yet He gave everything that you might be reconnected to the kind of rich, deep, abundant life found only in Him.

LIFE APPLICATION

Jesus' resurrection power is available to you. The Holy Spirit dwells inside you and makes it possible for you to live in a way that pleases God. The Great Exchange of your garbage for His righteousness is available to you every day, moment by moment, when you plug into the power of the Spirit.

Take a minute and thank Him for His resurrection power. Then invite the Spirit to come help you clean out one of those "sin closets" in your life that is still an ugly mess. Because the Great Exchange is the *real* gift that keeps on giving as we strive to live pure and holy lives for the glory of God!

34 THE "YOU MEAN TO TELL ME..." PEOPLE

Jesus said to them [the chief priests and the elders in the temple courts], *"Truly I tell you, the tax collectors and the prostitutes are entering the kingdom of God ahead of you. For John came to you to show you the way of righteousness, and you did not believe him, but the tax collectors and the prostitutes did. And even after you saw this, you did not repent and believe him.* Matthew 21:31b- 32

Like I mentioned in an earlier devo reading, Dare 2 Share gathered seven young strangers of diverse religious worldviews together for the spiritual reality series *GOSPEL Journey Maui.* Our group discussions focused around some of the great questions of life. Questions like: Is there a higher power? What is the purpose of life? Why do bad things happen? What happens after we die?

Over the course of the filming, I found it fascinating that two of the cast members, Jasser and Jonathan, were united on one thing: the outrageousness of the message of grace. You see, Jasser was a devout Muslim, while Jonathan was Jewish by heritage and agnostic by choice. Yet despite the cultural chasm between this Muslim and Jew, they found a common rallying cry when it came to Jesus' scandalous message of grace. When they realized that the Bible teaches salvation by faith and not by works, their response was surprisingly similar. Outrageous. Unfathomable. You mean to tell me... all it takes is faith in Jesus? It doesn't matter what you've done, how bad you've been...?

Jesus' scandalous message of grace never ceases to outrage. The religious leaders back in Jesus day were outraged too. They questioned and challenged His radical teachings about the grace and mercy of God. You can also most imagine them saying something like, "You mean to tell me...all a sinner has to do is put their trust in You..."

And Jesus' habit of hanging out with the "non-religious" crowd—tax collectors, prostitutes and sinners of all stripes—was scandalous beyond measure, too. Because the religious leaders of Jesus' day were all about their manmade traditions and "extra" laws, through which they had turned the Old Testament law into a onerous, burdensome list. And in the process, they had become petty, self-righteous rule enforcers who set themselves up as judge and jury to the Jewish people.

That's why the chief priests and elders so despised Jesus' teachings. His way of grace not only threatened their power over the people, but struck at the very core of how they viewed God and how they viewed themselves. What an affront to their pious sensibilities when Jesus told them point blank in Matthew 21 that *"the tax collectors and the prostitutes are entering the kingdom of God ahead of you."* Jesus is shifting the whole spiritual dynamic by declaring that God embraces those who seek after Him with a humble heart, knowing they're a sinner in need of God's grace, trusting only in their faith in Him.

Jesus' scandalous message of grace never ceases to outrage.

The religious folks found Jesus' message so outrageous that they decided He must be put to death.

And down through the intervening centuries, the scandalous message of the gospel has continued to outrage, for example, when mass murderer Jeffrey Dahmer was led to Christ by a prison minister. Dahmer killed 17 young men, so it grievously offends our human sense of right and wrong that he could be forgiven by God as a result of simply putting his faith in Christ.

Jesus' way of grace struck at the core of how they viewed God and themselves.

Even the great Apostle Paul, before He came to faith in Christ, was a Christian-hater (Acts 9:1) and zealously persecuted believers, including assenting to the stoning of Stephen for his faith in Christ (Acts 7). Paul referred to himself as the "chief of sinners." He knew all too well that his past behaviors would never earn him a place in heaven.

LIFE APPLICATION

Do you have someone in your life who you've given up on? We all have "difficult" people in our lives who need to be introduced to Jesus. Sometimes, if we've been hurt by someone over and over, our human tendency may be to write these kinds of people off as too far beyond the reach of God. But God says differently. Even mass murders are not beyond the reach of His grace.

Absolutely no one is beyond the reach of the grace of God. Do you *really* believe this statement? Talk to God about how it makes you feel. Angry? Hopeful? Or something else entirely? Then think of someone you've been feeling like it would take a miracle of God in order for them to come to faith in Jesus. Now pray for them. After all, God is in the miracle business. When you actually stop to think about, every single soul that's ever been blasted out of darkness and into His marvelous light IS a miracle.

LIFE

WITH JESUS
STARTS NOW AND LASTS **FOREVER**

Now this is eternal life:
that they know you, the only
true God, and Jesus Christ,
whom you have sent.

- John 17:3

35 QUALITY VS. QUANTITY

Now this is eternal life: that they know you, the only true God, and Jesus Christ, whom you have sent. John 17:3

What comes to mind when you think of "eternal life"? Heaven, God on His throne in all His grandeur? Seeing Jesus face-to-face? Angels, pearly gates, streets of gold, mansions with many rooms?

For many years of my life, my concept of "eternal life" was entirely focused on what happens after we die. When I talked to others about the gospel, I was all about that fateful determination of whether they would go to heaven or hell for all eternity, depending on whether or not they had put their faith and trust in Christ alone for their salvation. I was focused on the quantity of life and being with Jesus FOREVER.

And no doubt about it, this is an incredibly important dimension of eternal life with Christ.

But then I met my good friend, Zane Black, who was all about telling others about the abundant life that Jesus talks about in John 10:10 when He says, *"The thief comes only to steal and kill and destroy; I have come that they may have life, and have it to the full."* Zane loved to tell people about the quality of life available to them when they put their faith and trust in Jesus. And it's absolutely true that Jesus came to set us free from being "slaves to sin." You see, Zane had always lived life on the edge, looking for all the crazy excitement and adventure life has to offer. But he had ended up "going all in" for the wrong things. And it had almost cost him his life one night when he'd ended up in the hospital ER in an alcohol-induced coma.

But after years of living for cheap thrills and temporary highs, Zane experienced a radical encounter with Jesus that changed his life forever. So Zane is passionate about telling those who are struggling with life in the here and now about the freedom they can have in Christ NOW and about the new life and purpose faith in Jesus brings when we choose to follow Him.

Zane's perspective reminded me that God wants even more for us than "just" an eternity with Him in heaven after we die. We can experience "eternal life" from the very first moment we put our trust in Jesus. He came to set us free so that we no longer need to walk through our lives here on earth in bondage to sin. That's why Jesus describes eternal life as knowing *"the only true God and Jesus Christ."*

We must never reduce the gospel down to a self-help program.

And my perspective on heaven and hell reminded Zane that we must never reduce the message of the gospel and our life with Jesus down to a self-help program of "5 Steps to a Better Life Now." Of course, doing life with Jesus IS a far better way to do life, but the gospel is about far more than the here and now—it's about all of eternity!

Beautifully, it's **BOTH/AND**, because life with Jesus starts now and lasts forever.

LIFE APPLICATION
Reflect on these questions:

- Which do you tend to emphasize when you think about life with Jesus—quality or quantity?
- Does your perspective need to be rebalanced?
- Do you ever talk to others about eternal life? If not, why not?

Watch the short YouTube video "Then What?" found at <u>somethingamazing.net/then-what</u>. Consider sending the link as a conversation starter to someone who needs to get to know *"the only true God"* who offers eternal life that starts now and lasts forever.

36 "GOD'S MY DADDY!"

The Spirit you received does not make you slaves, so that you live in fear again; rather, the Spirit you received brought about your adoption to sonship. And by him we cry, "Abba, Father." The Spirit himself testifies with our spirit that we are God's children. Now if we are children, then we are heirs—heirs of God and co-heirs with Christ, if indeed we share in his sufferings in order that we may also share in his glory. Romans 8:15-17

Almost 65 years ago, the Korean War was raging and Toney was tapped on the shoulder to go fight for God and country. Toney had been a preacher, of sorts, as a young man, but being a soldier felt more like his divine calling.

As a sergeant in the Army, he fought valiantly. He was eventually captured by the North Koreans, and held as a Prisoner of War at Pyok-Dong. When Toney was finally released, he came back to his home town of Sacramento as a celebrated war hero. He decided to stick with the Army life, and eventually ascended to the rank of Sergeant Major.

But like so many military men, over the years, he turned to the party life. One day while out on the town, he met a girl named Shirley. They partied. She got pregnant. He found out and got transferred 2,000 miles away.

When he died a few years later, among the things he had left to show for his life were a brokenhearted family, a dusty Bible he'd preached from all those years ago, a few old medals from the war and a son he'd never met…me.

I'm the illegitimate son of Sergeant Major Toney Woods. I've never seen my father's face. I've never heard my father's voice. I don't know much about my biological father, other than what I just shared with you, and that he left me and my mom before I was even born.

He is our Papa, our Dada, our Pops!

But don't you dare feel sorry for me. Because I have another Daddy, a heavenly Father! And, if you're a believer in Jesus, then He's your Daddy, too!

You and I have been adopted into God's family.

Think about that. In the Roman culture, at the time of the writing of the epistles, if you were an adopted son, you would receive all the blessings, riches and rights as the natural sons in that family.

In the same way, we receive all the same blessings, riches and rights as Jesus. Now we can call God "Abba, Father." *Abba* is the Aramaic version of Daddy. He is our Papa, our Dada, our Pops! That may seem disrespectful, but it's not. It's a term of intimacy. The same sovereign, large and in charge King of kings and Lord of lords is our Papa, too.

Ten years ago, my mom went to be with the Lord. As she lay dying of lung cancer in hospice, over the course of 40 days and 40 nights, we had several great conversations. She asked me at one point, "Do you remember what you used to say to the kids in the neighborhood who would make fun of you for not having a dad?" I said, "No." She responded, "You used to say 'God's my daddy!'" I told her, "Ma, I don't remember saying that, but I remember feeling it from the moment I put my faith in Jesus."

And guess what? If you're a believer in Jesus, you are a child of God, too! He is your Daddy, and according to Hebrews 13:5, He will never leave you or forsake you!

About eight years ago, I got a really strange e-mail from some lady in Sacramento. It simply read, "I think I may be your sister. Is your dad named Toney Woods?" I responded to her in the affirmative.

Interestingly, this happened to be two days before I was scheduled to fly into Sacramento—to my recollection, for the first time in my life. So we set up a meeting time and place, and it was an instant family reunion. Marilyn was my sister, and I found out I had another brother and another sister.

You, too, have another family.

Little did I know that I had a whole other family. Our meeting was not awkward at all. Although I was the "embarrassing family secret" that had gotten spilled at a family reunion, after the only person in the know had downed too many drinks, they took me in like I'd known them all my life. Although my mom had been "the other woman," they still loved me.

You, too, have another family. God is your Daddy. And according to Hebrews 2:11, Jesus is your big brother. But your family is even bigger than that! According to Galatians 3:26, we are God's children through faith in Christ—siblings with God as our Daddy.

Let's enjoy our family reunions every Sunday (or maybe even Saturday night)! Let's fellowship with each other and honor our heavenly Father together. Then let's get out in the highways and byways and invite others to join the family, too, through faith in Christ.

LIFE APPLICATION

Do you think of God as your Daddy? If not, drill down into those feelings some. Then invite God the Father to more fully reveal that aspect of His character to you.

Do you know others who need to get a personal invitation from you to come meet your Daddy and your church family? There are lots of ways to bring God up in your conversations with your friends. Here are a few examples of questions you might ask to get the conversation going...

- What's most important to you in the whole world? (Consider using the short video found at somethingamazing.net.)
- Where do you turn when people let you down or hurt you? (Consider using the short YouTube video "What Makes for Good Relationships?" with this question. You can find it at the following link: somethingamazing.net/relationships.)
- Have you ever felt like you aren't valuable or lovable? (Consider using the short YouTube video "How Valuable Am I?" with this question. You can find it at the following link: somethingamazing.net/value.)

37 THE MILLION DOLLAR QUESTION

And he died for all, that those who live should no longer live for themselves but for him who died for them and was raised again. 2 Corinthians 5:15

Several years ago, I ran into two gang members in the food court at The Citadel Mall in Colorado Springs, Colorado. When I saw them, God moved in my heart to begin a conversation.

Both of these gang members were wearing the color red because they were members of the "Bloods." And both were way bigger than me—one guy looked like he could have played linebacker for the Denver Broncos. And, surprisingly, he was the one interested in talking, when the conversation turned toward Jesus.

He was riveted to every word I said. He stood there flexed and focused. When I explained the gospel, he was ready to respond. The conversation went something like this.

"Does that make sense?"

"Yes," he responded.

"Then would you like to put your faith in Jesus right now to forgive you for all your sins and receive the free gift of eternal life?" I asked.

"Yes," he replied.

Then I quizzed him to make sure he understood the gospel. I said, "So if I see you 10 years from now and ask you if you have eternal life, what are you going to say?"

He said, "Yes, I do."

"How do you know?" I asked.

"Because Jesus died for my sins and I trust in Him, not my good deeds to save me," was his spot-on response.

Jesus just offered you something way more valuable.

But I knew that God had placed me there in the middle of the food court as something more than a ticket puncher for a one way trip to heaven. I knew that God had way more for this guy, and it wasn't going to start when he died and went to heaven. Life with Jesus started from the moment he said "yes" to faith in Christ.

I wanted him to know the futility of the gangsta life, but I wanted to explain it in a way that would help him know that serving Jesus is a response that we have out of gratefulness, not guilt.

It was there that God gave me an illustration.

I asked him a hypothetical question. "What if I walked up to you and had a duffle bag full of cash. Let's say it contained one million dollars. Say I came right up to you, and offered it to you free of charge, with no strings attached. Would you take it?"

He thought for a second or two and said, "Yes, I would."

"After you took it, would you slap me in the face, push me to the ground, kick me and spit on me, and then walk away with the duffle bag?" I asked.

"No, I'd buy you a hamburger or something," he said, glancing around the mall food court.

"Why would you do that?" I probed.

"Because I'd be grateful for the free gift," he responded.

Then I drove to the point of the illustration. "Jesus just walked right into this food court and, through me explaining the gospel to you, offered you something way more valuable than one million dollars. He gave you eternal life. He gave you hope. He gave you forgiveness for your sins. Are you going to take His free gift, then spit in His face and walk away, or are going to serve Him?"

> He died for us, so we should live for Him.

"I'm gonna serve Him," he said with an expression of excitement.

"Why? Because you have to, in order to be a Christian?" I asked.

"No, because I'm grateful for His free gift," he replied.

"What does this mean for your gang life?" I asked.

"It's over," he stated bluntly.

In that one moment, in the middle of a food court, that gang member understood that serving Jesus is not something you have to do to earn, keep or prove your salvation, but something you get to do out of sheer gratefulness for your salvation.

As 2 Corinthians 5:15 reminds us, He died for us, so we should live for Him. It's not a "have to," but a "get to," in light of the duffle bag full of hope that He has passed on to us.

LIFE APPLICATION

Spend some time talking to God about the following passage in Philippians 3.

What is more, I consider everything a loss because of the surpassing worth of knowing Christ Jesus my Lord…I press on to take hold of that for which Christ Jesus took hold of me. Brothers and sisters, I do not consider myself yet to have taken hold of it. But one thing I do: Forgetting what is behind and straining toward what is ahead, I press on toward the goal to win the prize for which God has called me heavenward in Christ Jesus (Philippians 3:8a; 12b-14).

Do you consider everything else in life a loss compared to the wonder of knowing Jesus as your Lord?

Is there something you need to put behind you so you can shift your focus to the goal ahead?

38 ALL IN...WITH A SMILE

Therefore, I urge you, brothers and sisters, in view of God's mercy, to offer your bodies as a living sacrifice, holy and pleasing to God—this is your true and proper worship.
Romans 12:1

Glendo Reservoir in Glendo, Wyoming is famous for its cliffs. During my time as a middle school youth leader at Community Baptist Church in Arvada, Colorado, we would rally our teenagers and make the three and a half hour trek northward to Lone Tree Bible Camp.

It was all-out western. Wes, the camp leader, was a bronco-busting, bull-riding, whip-wielding Wildman. We killed and ate rattlesnakes, and finished the week of camp with a full on rodeo.

But the highlight of all the fun activities was cliff diving at Glendo Reservoir. The jump could range from eight feet to 85 feet, and everywhere in between.

It became a rite of passage event for many of the kids and counselors who came to camp. Now, I'm not much for jumping off cliffs. And somehow, I had always managed to escape making the jump. But one particular year, I got called on it. This time somebody had noticed that I wasn't participating. So a handful of teenagers started chanting, "Greg! Greg! Greg!" Soon the other students joined in, and my worst nightmare began to unfold. The other counselors joined the chant and soon a chorus was ringing. Somehow, that chorus gave me courage.

Fueled by the cheers of water-drenched teenagers and adults, I charged toward the cliff at break neck speed. And, with one giant leap, I catapulted into the great blue sky,

God is chanting your name.

with a great big smile on my face. All in. Totally committed. No turning back.

Problem was, I didn't know how to swim. But I hit the water with a splat, and somehow flailed my way to the shore, safe and sound.

All in...with a smile. And it's that same all in attitude that God's longing for us to embrace, spiritually speaking.

God was chanting your name—so to speak—when He used Paul to pen the book of Romans. He was chanting your name when He unpacked the horrors of depravity in Romans 1-3. He was chanting your name when He unveiled a salvation by grace through faith in Jesus in Romans 3-5. God was cheering you on when He used Paul to make clear the doctrines of sanctification and glorification in Romans 6-8, and when He unveiled the doctrine of election in Romans 9-11. As Paul's divinely inspired fingers penned the end of Romans chapter 11, the poetic prose bursts forth,

> *Oh, the depth of the riches of the wisdom and knowledge of God!*
> *How unsearchable his judgments,*
> *and his paths beyond tracing out!*
> *"Who has known the mind of the Lord?*
> *Or who has been his counselor?"*
> *"Who has ever given to God,*
> *that God should repay them?"*
> *For from him and through him and for him are all things.*
> *To him be the glory forever! Amen* (Romans 11:33-36).

By this time, it's almost as though all of heaven is chanting your name. They are chanting for you to, in view of God's mercy, go all in with a smile! It's right after this that Paul writes the classic words, *"I urge you, brothers and sisters, in view of God's mercy, to offer your bodies as a living sacrifice."*

Take the leap, and jump into the rolling waves of serving Him. He'll empower you to swim, and all of heaven will cheer.

Serving Jesus is not a "have to." It's a "get to." It's the great adventure, the extreme sport and that great leap that we can choose to participate in.

It's interesting to me that Paul's words here are to people he already calls brothers and sisters. He was asking fellow believers to go all in to serve Jesus with everything. Notice that he doesn't tell them they have to do this in order to be to be saved—because they already are saved.

> # Take the leap, and jump into the rolling waves of serving Him.

Instead, he reminds them of the greatness of salvation, and challenges them to jump into serving Jesus with a great big smile.

Sure, there are costs to count. Yes, you must die to yourself as you pick up your cross and follow Jesus. But remember, His yoke is easy and His burden is light (Matthew 11:30).

Go all in with a smile, not because you have to, but because He went all in for you.

Geronimo!

LIFE APPLICATION

Are you all in? If not, what's holding you back? Have a conversation with God about how you're currently using your time, talent and treasure. Then identify one thing in your life you're going to change.

39 "AMDG"

So whether you eat or drink or whatever you do, do it all for the glory of God.
1 Corinthians 10:31

I knew at a young age that I wanted to be a preacher someday. But God took me on a circuitous journey to get there. In my twenties, I spent seven years roofing houses.

I learned a lot of valuable lessons during those seven years, but here's one of the most important: *"Whatever you do, do it all for the glory of God."*

You see, my roofing bosses—two brothers who owned the roofing company I worked for—were wise and godly Christian men. In fact, they told every single employee they hired that whether or not they were a believer in Jesus, they needed to know that the company roofed every job for the glory of God. The bosses demanded excellence from their employees. We were all expected to roof like each and every roof was the very roof of Jesus Himself.

I'd gotten this speech, right along with the rest of crew, but I hadn't *really* taken it to heart. I was frustrated that my preacher ambitions hadn't come to fruition yet. My attitude and actions made it clear that I really didn't want to be dragging shingles around on a hot roof. I wanted to be in front of an adoring church crowd preaching God's Word.

So one day, one of the owners pulled me aside for a candid conversation. "Greg," he said, "I believe God has given you a gift for preaching, and I also believe that someday He will provide you with a job where you can use that gift with excellence. But right now," he went on, "God has given you a job as a roofer. And you need to buckle down and get serious about putting on roofs with excellence, for the glory of God. I know he is calling you to be a preacher *someday*. But he is calling you to be a roofer *today*."

He was absolutely right!

"Ad maiorem Dei gloriam inque hominum salute." This Latin phrase from St. Ignatius translates: "For the greater glory of God and salvation of humanity." I strive to live by this ancient maxim and have taken it on as my "life motto." I call it AMDG, for short.

Whether we're frustrated by our current life circumstances, or we're happy as clams, our motivation for living a meaningful Christian life should be birthed out of a deep desire to bring God maximum glory, and to see people transformed by the power of the gospel.

"For the greater glory of God and salvation of humanity."

But sometimes our motivations get muddy—or outright hijacked. We become self-motivated, rather than kingdom-motivated. We begin to reduce the Christian life to simply wanting to "feel good" about being a good person, or to "managing" our sin well so that we don't find ourselves splat in the middle of a messy, uncomfortable set of life circumstances. We slip into seeking God's hand, instead of seeking His heart.

All of us wrestle with these kinds of ulterior motives that sap the vibrancy of our relationship with Jesus, and suck us into simply going through the outward motions of the Christian life.

The Bible cautions in 1 Corinthians 4:5, *"…wait until the Lord comes. He will bring to light what is hidden in darkness and will expose the motives of the heart."* So it's important that we honestly evaluate our motives and convictions.

AMDG—God's glory and the salvation of humanity—should drive everything we are and do. It should be the focal point of our work, our relationships, our pleasures and struggles. Everything.

We slip into seeking God's hand, instead of seeking His heart.

LIFE APPLICATION

Here are three steps to help you refocus your life around AMDG:

1. **Seek.** Take some time this week and prayerfully examine your heart. Honestly assess how you are doing when it comes to living an AMDG life.
2. **Share.** Share your assessment with a trusted friend or mentor. Talk about your struggles and challenges and your desire to grow and change so that your life can become more God-honoring and Gospel-advancing. Ask them to pray for you and hold you accountable.
3. **Cling.** Lean on the presence and power of Christ, as you strive to keep your motives pure and pleasing to the Lord. Ask God to help you plug into the power of the Holy Spirit moment by moment, so you can see your world through spiritual eyes and walk in His strength. Serving Him is not a matter of what you can do for God, rather, it's about what He can do through you. Learn to walk moment by moment in utter dependence on the Spirit who dwells within you.

There's not a single moment of a single day that we should consider "wasted time." Absolutely everything we're about should go through the AMDG grid!

40 BEST NEWS EVER

How, then, can they call on the one they have not believed in? And how can they believe in the one of whom they have not heard? And how can they hear without someone preaching to them? And how can anyone preach unless they are sent? As it is written: "How beautiful are the feet of those who bring good news!" Romans 10:14-15

On December 26th, 2004, the world was shaken by the most devastating earthquake in four decades. Massive waves destroyed entire villages and swept away tens of thousands of people from India to Indonesia. All together, over 200,000 people in 13 countries died in this massive catastrophe. I wept with the rest of the world as I watched replay after replay of the absolute and total devastation that swept up so many lives that day.

But it wasn't until recently that I heard the story of Tilley Smith, a 10-year-old girl from England who saved an entire beach full of people. Just two weeks before Tilley and her family had headed off to Thailand for a beach resort vacation, her geography teacher had done a unit on earthquakes and tsunamis.

On that fateful day, Tilley was the only one in her family to notice the warning signs. Though her mom was initially skeptical, Tilley's urgent adamancy that disaster was coming finally convinced her mom, dad and sister to head for safety. Her dad convinced the security guards, and they convinced the people on the beach that danger was imminent. One hundred people's lives were saved that day because Tilley sounded the alarm. [6]

Who are you going to convince? Because a tsunami called hell is headed straight toward those who don't know Jesus.

Sometimes, it seems like we Christians are so busy making sand castles and enjoying the view from where we sit, that we've forgotten the urgency of the message we carry that brings life and hope.

I'm not talking about going out in the streets and screaming at people that they're in danger of going to hell, or yelling at them to "turn or burn." I'm talking about lovingly, relationally and relentlessly bringing God up in real conversations. I'm talking about urgently sharing Jesus' message of hope with a desperate world.

We've forgotten the urgency of the message we carry.

The famous preacher Charles Spurgeon put it like this, "If sinners will be damned, at least let them leap to hell over our bodies. And if they will perish, let them perish with our arms around their knees, imploring them to stay…let no one go there unwarned and unprayed for." [7]

God has placed you as an early warning system in your neighborhood, at your job, at your school, in your family, in your circle of friends. You're there to encourage others to run into the safe arms of Jesus.

By sharing the love of Christ in word and deed, you're extending the lifeline they need to grab hold of in order to escape both the despair of a life without Jesus now, and eternity apart from Him forever.

You must always remember that when you share the good news of Jesus Christ, you are sharing the best news ever! For there's life and hope in these six simple words. God. Our. Sins. Paying. Everyone. Life.

God created us to be with Him.

Our sins separate us from God.

Sins cannot be removed by good deeds.

Paying the price for sin, Jesus died and rose again.

Everyone who trusts in Him alone has eternal life.

Life with Jesus starts now and lasts forever.

Those in danger of drowning won't be able to grab hold of the gospel and believe it, if they don't ever hear it. Like the Apostle Paul said, *"How will they hear without someone preaching to them?"*

LIFE APPLICATION

I encourage you to memorize the GOSPEL acrostic so that you will always be ready to share Jesus' message of hope anytime, anywhere, with anyone. It's an investment of effort that will stick with you for the rest of your life. And one that may impact others for all eternity.

Keep in mind that this six part acrostic is not intended to be a script, but simply a guide for your gospel conversations—something that helps you walk others through the message of the gospel in a simple, clear, concise, compelling way.

I like to compare it to learning to play a musical instrument. When you learn the GOSPEL acrostic, it's much like putting in the prep-work needed to play a guitar. First you learn the chords, because chords give you the basics you need to be creative and play your own personal, powerful, beautiful music. Similarly, the GOSPEL acrostic provides you the basics you need to share the beautiful message of the gospel personally and powerfully.

So master your chords, and pray for opportunities to share the best news ever with others.

Because heaven and hell hang in the balance.

ENDNOTES

[1] Rodgers, Fred M., *It's You I Like*, PBSKids.org, http://pbskids.org/rogers/songLyricsIt-sYouILike.html.

[2] Wikiquote.org, Fred Rodgers Quotes, Testimony before U.S. Senate committee, May 1, 1969. Featured in *Fred Rogers: America's Favorite Neighbor* (television documentary), 2003, http://en.wikiquote.org/wiki/Fred_Rogers.

[3] Cornwell, Erin York, Linda J. Waite, "Social Disconnectedness, Perceived Isolation, and Health among Older Adults." http://www.ncbi.nlm.nih.gov/pmc/articles/PMC2756979.

[4] Schaffer, Francis, *The Complete Works of Francis A Schaffer: A Christian Worldview*, Vol. 3, *True Spirituality* (Westchester, IL: Crossway Books, 1982), page 203.

[5] Spurgeongems.org, *Charles Spurgeon Sermons*, "A Sight of Self," Vol. 8, Sermon #437, page 5, http://www.spurgeongems.org/vols7-9/chs437.pdf.

[6] Harrison, Everett F., Geoffrey W. Bromiley, Carl F. H. Henry, eds., *Baker Dictionary of Theology*. Grand Rapids, MI: Baker, 1960, page 533.

[7] BBCNews.co, "Award for Tsunami Warning Pupil," September 9, 2005. http://news.bbc.co.uk/2/hi/uk/4229392.stm.

[8] Goodreads.com, *Charles H. Spurgeon Quotes*, http://www.goodreads.com/quotes/74181-if-sinners-be-damned-at-least-let-them-leap-to.

ABOUT THE AUTHOR

Greg Stier is founder and president of Dare 2
Share Ministries (D2S), a ministry that equips
teenagers to relationally share their faith. Greg
has spoken to and trained hundreds of thousands
of teens and adults in the last 20 years. A former
Pastor, church planter and youth leader, Greg is
the author of 15 books and numerous curriculum.
He has been married to his wife, Debbie, for 24
years. They have two children.

D2S also provides free online resources and a variety of curriculum, books and other
training resources for students and youth leaders. For more information about Dare 2
Share's resources and training conferences, please visit www.dare2share.org.

DARE 2 SHARE

Dare 2 Share believes in the power of the gospel and the potential of teenagers.

The gospel changes everything.

It saves lost souls and lost causes. When a teenager puts their faith in Jesus, they not only experience the power of God's love and forgiveness, but the power of His cause - to reach others with the good news of Jesus.

Dare 2 Share unleashes the potential of teenagers by inspiring and equipping them to reach their peers with the gospel.

By creating captivating training events and faith-sharing resources, hundreds of thousands of teenagers have been mobilized to reach their world for Jesus. Youth ministries across the nation have experienced accelerated spiritual growth as a result.

For more information about Dare 2 Share,
go to **www.dare2share. org**

RESOURCES FROM DARE 2 SHARE

FAITH-SHARING TOOLS AT YOUR FINGERTIPS

This mobile app will help train and inspire you to share your faith with your friends wherever you go!

Go to **dare2share.org/mobileapp** to download the FREE Dare 2 Share app.

AN EASY WAY TO BRING GOD UP WITH FRIENDS

Life in 6 Words

by Greg Stier

Using the six words of the GOSPEL— God, Our, Sins, Paying, Everyone, Life— *Life in 6 Words* clearly communicate Jesus' invitation to trust in Him.

This short, compelling, visually dynamic book is a perfect evangelism tool for relationally engaging others with the gospel of grace.

These and other great resources available at **www.dare2share.org**